THE MEDIA, THE COURT, AND THE MISREPRESENTATION

The Court's decisions are interpreted and disseminated via the media. During this process, the media paints an image of the Court and its business. Like any artist, the media has license regarding what to cover and the amount of attention devoted to any aspect of the Court and its business. Some cases receive tremendous attention, while others languish on the back pages or are ignored. These selection effects create a skewed picture of the Court and its work, and might affect public attitudes toward the Court. Indeed, studies of media coverage of other governmental institutions reveal that when, and how, their policy decisions are covered has implications for the public's understanding of, compliance with, support for, and cynicism about the policy.

This book uncovers and describes this coverage and compares it to the confirmation hearings, the Court's actual work, even its members. Rorie Spill Solberg and Eric N. Waltenburg analyze media coverage of nominations and confirmation hearings, the justices' "extra-curricular" activities and their retirements/deaths, and the Court's opinions, and compare this coverage to analyses of confirmation transcripts and the Court's full docket. Solberg and Waltenburg contend that the media now cover the Court and its personnel more similarly to its coverage of other political institutions. Journalists still regurgitate a mythology supported by the justices, a "cult of the robe," wherein unbiased and apolitical judges mechanically base their decisions upon the law and the Constitution. Furthermore, they argue the media also focus on the "cult of personality," wherein the media emphasize certain attributes of the justices and their work to match the public's preferences for subject matter and content. The media's portrayal, then, may undercut the Court's legitimacy and its reservoir of good will.

Rorie Spill Solberg is an associate professor in the School of Public Policy at Oregon State University. She is widely published in journals such as *Political Research Quarterly, Social Science Quarterly, Policy Studies Quarterly*, and the *Journal of Empirical Legal Studies*. In 2011, she was selected to edit *Judicature*, the journal of the American Judicature Society. She received her PhD in American politics with a specialty in judicial politics from The Ohio State University in 1997.

Eric N. Waltenburg is an associate professor of political science at Purdue University. His research interests concern judicial politics and state politics. He has published in such journals as *American Politics Research, Political Behavior*, and *Social Science Quarterly*, and he is the author or co-author of three books on judicial politics. He is a co-editor of *Politics, Groups, and Identities*, the official journal of the Western Political Science Association. He received his PhD from The Ohio State University in 1994 in American politics, with a focus on judicial politics.

Law, Courts and Politics

Edited by Robert M. Howard, Georgia State University

In *Democracy in America*, Alexis de Tocqueville famously noted that "scarcely any political question arises in the United States that is not resolved, sooner or later, into a judicial question." The importance of courts in settling political questions in areas ranging from health care to immigration shows the continuing astuteness of de Tocqueville's observation. To understand how courts resolve these important questions, empirical analyses of law, courts, and judges, and the politics and policy influence of law and courts have never been more salient or more essential.

Law, Courts and Politics was developed to analyze these critically important questions. This series presents empirically driven manuscripts in the broad field of judicial politics and public law by scholars in law and social science. It uses the most up to date scholarship and seeks an audience of students, academics, upper division undergraduate and graduate courses in law, political science, and sociology as well as anyone interested in learning more about law, courts, and politics.

1. **The Dual System of Privacy Rights in the United States**
   Mary McThomas

2. **Making Law and Courts Research Relevant**
   Brandon L. Bartels and Chris W. Bonneau

3. **Europeanization of Judicial Review**
   Nicola Ch. Corkin

4. **The Media, the Court, and the Misrepresentation**
   The New Myth of the Court
   Rorie Spill Solberg and Eric N. Waltenburg

THE MEDIA, THE COURT, AND THE MISREPRESENTATION

The New Myth of the Court

By Rorie Spill Solberg and Eric N. Waltenburg

NEW YORK AND LONDON

First published 2015
by Routledge
711 Third Avenue, New York, NY 10017

and by Routledge
2 Park Square, Milton Park, Abingdon, Oxon OX14 4RN

Routledge is an imprint of the Taylor & Francis Group, an informa business

© 2015 Taylor & Francis

The right of Rorie Spill Solberg and Eric N. Waltenburg to be identified as authors of this work has been asserted by them in accordance with sections 77 and 78 of the Copyright, Designs and Patents Act 1988.

All rights reserved. No part of this book may be reprinted or reproduced or utilized in any form or by any electronic, mechanical, or other means, now known or hereafter invented, including photocopying and recording, or in any information storage or retrieval system, without permission in writing from the publishers.

Trademark notice: Product or corporate names may be trademarks or registered trademarks, and are used only for identification and explanation without intent to infringe.

Library of Congress Cataloging-in-Publication Data

Solberg, Rorie Spill, 1969– author.

The media, the court, and the misrepresentation : the new myth of the court / Rorie L. Solberg, Eric N. Waltenburg.
    pages cm. — (Law, courts and politics ; 4)
  Includes bibliographical references and index.
  1. United States. Supreme Court—Press coverage—United States.
2. Courts of last resort—Press coverage—United States. 3. Judicial process—United States. I. Waltenburg, Eric N., 1965– author. II. Title.
  KF8748.S538 2014
  347.73'26—dc23   2014025500

ISBN: 978-0-415-82337-1 (hbk)
ISBN: 978-1-138-83123-0 (pbk)
ISBN: 978-0-203-55172-1 (ebk)

Typeset in Bembo
by Apex CoVantage, LLC

Printed and bound in the United States of America by Publishers Graphics, LLC on sustainably sourced paper.

CONTENTS

List of Figures and Tables		*ix*
1	Introduction: The Myths of the Court	1
2	Confirmation and the "Cult of Personality"	12
3	The Decisional Myth	37
4	The Decisional Myth, Part 2—The Landmark Cases	57
5	The Personal Myth	85
6	Conclusion: Processing the Myths of the Court	106
Index		*115*

FIGURES AND TABLES

Figures

2.1	Categories Accounting for at Least Five Percent of the Mentions in Confirmation Hearings	21
2.2	Categories Accounting for at Least Five Percent of the Mentions in Confirmation Hearings by Party	22
2.3	Distribution of Categories for Roberts Hearings	24
2.4	Distribution of Categories for Alito Hearings	24
2.5	Distribution of Categories for Sotomayor Hearings	25
2.6	Distribution of Categories for Kagan Hearings	25
2.7	Distribution of Categories: Media Reports on Senators	27
2.8	Distribution of Categories: Media Reports on Nominees	28
2.9	Distribution of Categories: Reporter-Led Information	29
2.10	Distribution of Categories: Media Coverage of Roberts Hearings	31
2.11	Distribution of Categories: Media Coverage of Alito Hearings	31
2.12	Distribution of Categories: Media Coverage of Sotomayor Hearings	32
2.13	Distribution of Categories: Media Coverage of Kagan Hearings	32
3.1	Distribution of Supreme Court Output, Various Terms	39
3.2	Aggregate Word Cloud Issue Distribution of Docket	46
3.3	Aggregate Word Cloud Issue Distribution of News Stories	47
3.4	Mean References to Justices' Personal or Political Information per Story	53
5.1a	Distribution of First Mentions: Justice Harry Blackmun	88
5.1b	Distribution of First Mentions: Justice John Paul Stevens	88
5.1c	Distribution of Second Mentions: Justice Harry Blackmun	91

x Figures and Tables

5.1d	Distribution of Second Mentions: Justice John Paul Stevens	91
5.2	Increase in Probability of Second Mention	92
5.3	Increase in Probability of "Cult of Personality" Mention	93
5.4	Total Mentions over Time: Justices Blackmun and Stevens	94
5.5	Total Mentions of Court Work and Non-Court Work: Justices Blackmun and Stevens	96
5.6	Focus of Media Storm Stories	98

Tables

2.1	Substantive Coverage, Proportion of Categories: Hearings vs. Media Reports	29
3.1	Distribution of Court Output by Issue Area	40
3.2	Total Unique Cases Covered by Medium	41
3.3a	Total Stories and Unique Docket Numbers for October Term 1975	42
3.3b	Total Stories and Unique Docket Numbers for October Term 1985	42
3.3c	Total Stories and Unique Docket Numbers for October Term 1989	43
3.3d	Total Stories and Unique Docket Numbers for October Term 1996	44
3.3e	Total Stories and Unique Docket Numbers for October Term 2006	44
3.3f	Total Stories and Unique Docket Numbers for October Term 2009	45
3.4	News Pegs by Term and Newspaper	48
3.5	Average Number of Sentences per Story, Content of the Decision	51
4.1	*CQ* Landmark Cases	59
4.2	Frequency of Media Coverage of Landmark Cases	62
4.3	Mean Sentences per Story: Landmark vs. Non-Landmark Decisions	63
5.1	Three Types of Readers	100

1

INTRODUCTION: THE MYTHS OF THE COURT

It stands majestic—four stories tall, longer and wider than a football field, and built almost entirely of gleaming marble from three continents. Huge statues guard the stairs leading to its main entrance—on the left, a female holding a book of laws and a small set of scales (the *Contemplation of Justice*); on the right, a male with a tablet of laws and a sheathed sword (the *Authority of Law*). At the top of the stairs, 16 Greek Corinthian columns support the pediment. "Equal Justice Under Law" is inscribed on the architrave. Capping this entrance is a sculpture group of six figures representing liberty, order, and authority. Bronze doors weighing six and a half tons allow entry into the main corridor, known as the "Great Hall," on either side of which are double rows of columns rising high to a coffered ceiling. At the Great Hall's east end, oak doors open into the "Court Chamber." The area of this room is over 7,500 square feet, and has a ceiling that rises 44 feet above the floor. It is a study in marble and mahogany. Twenty-four marble columns stand inside. The Chamber's walls are marble and covered with friezes, and there are marble borders along the floor. The raised bench—which is the room's focal point—and the other furniture are mahogany. The room, like the building itself, is opulent, designed to communicate gravity, stature, and prestige. This "Marble Palace" is the structural equivalent of the "cult of the robe" and supports the "myth of legality."

The "myth of legality" is the belief that the law, precedent, and fidelity to the Constitution alone guide the Supreme Court's decisions (Gibson and Caldeira 2009; Scheb and Lyons 2000). The justices, in turn, are seen as both legal technicians, apolitical and objective arbiters of the Constitution, and guardians of that "sacred text." According to the myth, the justices arrive at their decisions impartially, free of the influence of political and/or ideological biases.[1] In short, the justices operate "above" the bare knuckles of the political process. To be sure, through their rulings, the justices create winners and losers and determine who gets what,

2 Introduction: The Myths of the Court

when, and how much of society's finite resources. But despite the Court being enmeshed in politics, the public's subscription to the "legal myth" helps to ensure that the Court is perceived "as a uniquely nonpolitical political institution" (Gibson and Caldeira 2011, 200).

Myths are important and useful things in politics. Widely shared and usually uncritically accepted legends or stories, political myths explain or rationalize the political process (see Fiscus 1991, 314). Thus, they orient how the citizenry perceives the various aspects of its political system and that system's outputs. Moreover, since myths typically have positive connotations—often suggesting power, virtue, or some sort of divine beneficence—that understanding engenders support for the political system or at least tolerance for its outputs. In other words, political myths contribute to the political system's legitimacy (on the legitimacy of political regimes, see Easton 1965). This legitimizing effect is certainly the case for the "myth of legality" and the U.S. Supreme Court.

Lacking any truly coercive power, the Supreme Court is dependent upon the good will of the public to accept, and the other political institutions to implement, its policy decisions. But why should they? The answer seems to lie in the special place the Constitution occupies among the American public and the close association the "myth of legality" creates between the Court, the decisions of the justices, and the Constitution. First, according to Clawson and Waltenburg constitutionalism approaches a "secular religion" among the American public (2009, 56). Consequently, policies—even unpopular ones—are more likely to be accepted, or at least tolerated, if they are deemed to be constitutional. Second, as Charles Evans Hughes once said, "We are under a Constitution, but the Constitution is what the judges say it is." In other words, the American political system has vested in the judiciary "the power to play God" with respect to fundamental constitutional issues. This, in turn, necessitated the creation of "myths to sustain and rationalize this awesome exercise of power" (Segal, Spaeth, and Benesh 2005, 16–17). According to the "cult of the robe," the justices are oracles, simply giving voice to the Constitution. Their rulings (i.e., the Court's decisions), therefore, *are* the Constitution (Segal, Spaeth, and Benesh 2005, 16). As a result, the public and other actors in the political system are predisposed to accept and abide by the Court's policy pronouncements (Clawson, Kegler, and Waltenburg 2003; Clawson and Waltenburg 2009). After all, the Court's statements and the Constitution, according to the myth that has been woven to rationalize the Court's power, are one and the same.

Not surprisingly, given the institutional clout the "cult of the robe" affords the Court, the justices work to promote it by dressing their actions in the legalistic trappings that are so central to it (Epstein and Knight 1998). Justice Owen Roberts, for example, when striking down a key piece of New Deal legislation, bottomed his opinion on the "cult of the robe." "When an Act of Congress is appropriately challenged in the courts as not conforming to the constitutional mandate, the judicial branch of the government has only one duty—to lay the article of the Constitution which is invoked beside the statute which is challenged and decide whether the latter squares with the former" (*U.S. v. Butler*, 297 U.S. 1 at 62 [1936]). Furthermore, it is not unusual for the justices "to present themselves to the public through the media as legal scholars and authorities rather than politicians" (Baird and Gangl 2006, 599; see also the sources cited therein).

But it is not only the justices who, in their institutional interest, promote the "cult of the robe." Actors from the other political institutions promulgate the view that the Court and the justices are (or should be) above politics as well. In 1939, Senator Frank Murphy, for example, declared that "Members of the Supreme Court are not called upon nor expected to represent any specific interest or group, area, or class of persons" (qtd. in O'Brien 1996, 85–86). More recently, Senator Orrin Hatch, explaining his support for Ruth Bader Ginsburg's confirmation to the Supreme Court, emphasized the *constitutionality* and therefore apolitical nature of Ginsburg's decisions. "Her judicial record demonstrates that she is willing and able to issue rulings called for by the Constitution and the Federal statutes, even though Judge Ginsburg, were she a legislator, might personally have preferred different results as a matter of policy" (*Cong. Rec.*, August 2, 1993, 18132). Presidents typically explain their choice of nominee in terms of the nominee's fidelity to the Constitution and legal expertise. President Bush, for example, declared that he chose John Roberts to replace Chief Justice Rehnquist because of the former's "deep reverence for the Constitution, . . . and his complete devotion to the cause of justice" (Stevenson 2005). And when announcing Elena Kagan's nomination, President Obama described her as "one of the nation's foremost *legal* minds" (Rowland 2010 [emphasis ours]).

Traditionally, the Fourth Estate has been no less likely to espouse the "myth of legality" in its portrayal of the Court (Spill and Oxley 2003). To a degree, of course, this is a function of the press's reliance on the statements of its sources about the Court. Given the prevalence of the "cult of the robe," it would be expected that the lion's share of those sources would couch their references to the Court in terms of its apolitical and impartial nature. In addition, the press's heavy use of the Court's *own* language in its reports of the Court's actions (a mode of press behavior consistent with a media norm of reliance upon "official," authoritative sources; see Bennett 1996; Gans 1979) helps to ensure the Court is presented as an institution separate from politics. After all, the Court does not refer to itself as a "political institution" in its opinions, and it grounds its decisions in such "objective" criteria as fidelity to the Constitution and precedent (Davis 1994, 20; see also Entman and Paletz 1980).

But it is not just the press's use of sources that helps to dress the Court in the legal myth. To some degree, Court reporters have promoted the legal myth as well. Davis notes that many journalists perceive the Court as an institution critical to American democracy for its role in safeguarding minority rights, and therefore

4 Introduction: The Myths of the Court

they feel obliged to protect its institutional legitimacy. "This attitude produces a willingness to allow the institution to define itself in terms most favorable to itself" (Davis 1994, 128).

The "cult of the robe," then, overhangs the media's stories about the Court. As Hall Jamieson and Waldman point out, however, these stories appearing in newspapers and on television "are not called 'stories' by accident" (2003, 1). They are artistic constructions of reality. And like any artistic expression there is license or discretion used in terms of what to cover and how much attention to bestow on that subject. Consequently, "certain types of stories will be selected, while others will not." And this is not without consequence. "There is thus a strong possibility that there will be systematic differences between news content and the real world" (Soroka 2012, 515).

Indeed, we hypothesize that this artistic license has helped to usher in a new myth of the Court. Specifically, a variety of conditions (modern media norms, developments with respect to the Court) have come together that, when coupled with the reporters' license suggested by Hall Jamieson and Waldman, has bent the media's orientation about what is reported on the Court and what is deemed to be "newsworthy." This new myth emphasizes the justices' personalities—their ideological and legal philosophies as well as elements of their life stories—and attaches newsworthiness to events and facts that involve the individual justice. Thus, for example, nominations, confirmations, and departures command the media's attention about the Court. They function as "news pegs," affecting the public's understanding and knowledge of the Court. Accordingly, about the only time the public hears a focused accounting of the nature of the Court's business is during Senate confirmation hearings. And since certain topics "sell" better than others, the media coverage of modern confirmations indicates that an issue dominating the Court's attention involves privacy and its relationship to the question of abortion. Consequently, the public's understanding of the nature of the Court's caseload is skewed.

Oftentimes, even stories about decisions are reported in a way that connects them to the personality of a justice. Cases involving abortion and Justice Blackmun are perhaps the most obvious example, but the stories about Chief Justice Roberts's opinion upholding the *Patient Protection and Affordable Care Act* ("Obamacare") as a means to preserve the Court's public esteem are also examples of this mode of reporting on the Court.[2]

This new myth of the "cult of personality" is consistent with modern journalistic norms of personalization, drama, and novelty (Boykoff and Boykoff 2007, 1192). It permits reporters to attach a human element to the Court's decisional outputs by connecting them to the identities of certain justices—Blackmun, for example, leading the diminished Court liberals and turning back the various assaults on *Roe*, warning that at some point he would no longer be there to defend the precedent,[3] or Roberts sacrificing his conservative credentials in order to "save" the Court.[4] It injects drama by emphasizing the tone of the justices' opinions: "There was a blistering dissenting opinion written by Justice Byron R. White,"[5] or by noting conflict over decisions such as President Obama's televised criticism of *Citizens United* and Justice Alito's mouthed "Not true" during the State of the Union.[6] And there are few events more novel than a retirement from or appointment to the Court.

The "cult of personality" also plays well with the modern media's attention to celebrity as the focus of the news (Davis 2011, 27), and it seems part and parcel with what one keen observer of the relationship between the press and the Court has identified as a changed media environment. Richard Davis notes that since the 1960s professional journalism has adopted a different approach to coverage of the political system, one that is more aggressive, challenging, and investigatory. The consequences for the Court seem to be that journalists are more likely to perceive it as a political institution inhabited not by philosopher kings but by individuals with personal and political motivations (2011, 25–27). Identifying and reporting on these motivations has increased the incidence of journalists making references to the justices' ideological dispositions and/or their life stories as explanations. Davis quotes the Associated Press reporter, Richard Carelli, on this point:

> When Justice Stevens writes an opinion about parental rights, we can put in the story that this author is himself the adoptive parent of two children. It adds something for the readers, an appreciation of where this guy is coming from. (Davis 1994, 103)

Thus, recognized media practices and a new style of journalism have played a role in the rise of the "cult of personality." But several other developments, more central to the Court, have helped to usher it in as well. First, since at least the 1950s, the Court has been involved in especially divisive social issues touching on race relations and privacy that have increasingly made it the object of controversy and political contest. This in turn has increased the likelihood of referring to the Court and politics in the same breath. Whether a cause or a symptom, the Court's footprints in these issue areas are associated with a perception among some reporters that the Court is "plainly a political institution. Behind the black robes and the legal mumbo-jumbo are nine politicians who are making public policy as well as law" (Davis 1994, 126).

Of course this perception (recognition) is not limited to the journalists covering the Court. Organized interests are very aware of it as well, and whether in pursuit of policy or to propagandize for members and resources, organized interests have located their energies in the Supreme Court with increasing frequency. One of the strategies these groups employ is to act as a source for the media reporting the Court's decisions, and as sources, groups attempt to frame the Court's decisions in a manner most advantageous to their objectives. In this effort,

6 Introduction: The Myths of the Court

they might well be less likely to emphasize the traditional legal myth surrounding the Court and more likely to cast the Court as just another political institution and the justices as just another set of politicians.[7] Consequently, the increased activity of organized interests in the judiciary has yielded additional information for journalists to draw upon, information that contributes to the "cult of personality" (see Davis 1994, 100–1).

The nomination and confirmation process has changed dramatically over this time period as well, transforming from a standard, even sleepy constitutional procedure to something more akin to a political campaign, with all the attendant smoke and fire. Here again, organized interests have a noteworthy presence. To begin, they affect the very nature of the individual nominated. Once a nominee or potential nominee is made public, they conduct background research and provide information on the nominee for both the Senate and the media. And they mount public opinion operations in the hopes of affecting a nominee's fate (Davis 2005, 106–10, 112). Efforts are made to construct the most appealing (or disturbing) personal story about a nominee, depending upon which side of the nomination battle the entity constructing the story falls. As Davis points out, the "story defines the nominee in a way that enhances public appeal and makes confirmation more likely, because senators are unlikely to want to oppose a nominee with an alluring personal story" (2005, 132). A story that wreaks havoc on a nominee's public image, on the other hand, is likely to sink the nominee in the Senate. And of course the press is enlisted in communicating these stories to both the Senate and the public (Davis 2005, 142–45).

Thus, the modern nomination and confirmation process generates significant amounts of information about the eventual justice that is much more personal in nature, and that is distinctive from the justices' traditional portrayal as "priests of the robe." What is more, since the appointment process has taken on the hues of an electoral campaign, with the associated political pyrotechnics—demonstrations, framing wars carried out in the op-ed pages, the opportunity for bombshell personal stories to be unearthed—nominations and confirmations appeal strongly to the business imperatives of the media (Davis 2005, 117–18). Conflict is likely, and the press is on hand to capture it. During the appointment process, then, all the conditions are present to facilitate the construction of the "cult of personality." Actors intent on constructing and propagandizing personal stories about a nominee are paired with a press seeking drama and eager to report it.

Finally, some of the justices have become more willing to open their lives to the press and public in biographies and autobiographies, speeches and interviews. Whether to better inform the public about the powerful and mysterious institution in which they act, or to shape the historical record about themselves, several of the justices are simply more public (see Davis 2011, especially chapter 7). And this too has facilitated the rise of the "cult of personality."

Expectations and Plan for the Book

Since the mass media is the primary source of the public's information about the Supreme Court (Caldeira 1986; Franklin and Kosaki 1995), it is important to understand how the media portrays the Court. After all, in the end, how the public views the Court depends a great deal on the media's depiction both of it and its members (see Christenson and Glick 2014; Gibson and Caldeira 2009; Gibson, Caldeira, and Baird 1998; Johnston and Bartels 2010). If, as others argue, the reservoir of public support for the Court ebbs and flows depending upon the public's perception of the Court's work, then it is critical to understand how that perception is built.

The modern media's representation of the Court has always been distorted. Historically, it has processed its stories about the Court through the lens of the legal myth, and this certainly has inoculated, bolstered, and preserved the Court's institutional legitimacy with respect to the mass public. But it has also engendered an invalid understanding of the Court's work and the behavior of the justices. (Given its effect on legitimacy, whether this understanding is good or bad is open to debate.) We hypothesize that for several reasons a different lens through which the media views the Court and the justices has developed over the course of the past several decades. This new lens focuses on the justices as personalities, their legal and ideological philosophies, and their life stories.

Now, if this new lens, this "cult of personality," is in fact orienting the media's coverage of the Court, we should observe certain patterns in how the media covers the Court and the justices. First, we expect that media coverage of the confirmation process will concentrate either on senatorial questions concerning only a few types of issues that appear in the Court, those issues most freighted with drama and potential conflict and that involve a clash of philosophies or moral ideals, or those questions that would most likely elicit compelling personal, life-story information about the nominee. Second, we expect the media's coverage of the Court's decisional outputs to be incomplete and potentially misleading. Certain types of cases and controversies are more likely to be reported, and those reports will place the Court in a storyline draped in politics, with the attendant focus on winners and losers, and strategic or tactical considerations. Finally, we expect that coverage of individual justices across their careers will be unbalanced. Appreciable attention will be paid to the justice at the beginning and end of his or her career on the High Bench. Between these bookend moments, however, justices will be relatively anonymous, unless they are connected at a personal level with a given type of issue.

These expectations are subject to empirical testing and in the chapters that follow we do just that. We begin in chapter 2 with an exploration of the mythology that develops around the confirmation process. The media begins

8 Introduction: The Myths of the Court

to mischaracterize the Court and its work from this early stage forward, and so begins to build the new myth of the Court. In this chapter, we examine the four most recent Supreme Court nomination hearings (John Roberts, Samuel Alito, Sonia Sotomayor, and Elena Kagan). We analyze the transcripts for each day of questioning of the nominee, coding each question for its substantive content, the answer, as well as information about the senator who posed the question. We also collect newspaper articles and television broadcast transcripts covering the hearings. Again, we code the article for substantive content including subjects and senatorial mentions. After summarizing these data separately, we compare the coverage with the actual content of the hearings to show how skewed the media's coverage is. We find that the media's coverage focuses on only a few of the 19 members sitting on the Judiciary Committee. Furthermore, *based upon the media reports*, the only items of concern to the Senate are the nominee's fealty to precedent, the status of *Roe*, and the compelling personal biography of the nominee. This coverage suggests that these items are the most important for the senators in their analysis of the nominee and that privacy and its relationship to the questions of abortion are the only important issues before the Court.

In chapter 3 we examine the coverage of the Court and its decisions for six terms of the Court using a pseudo rolling cross-section methodology. These "years in the life" typify certain time periods, Courts, and personalities. The methodology we employ is similar to that used by Spill and Oxley (2003), and using it we are able to explore variation in the media's coverage of the Court's merits decisions both across the type of media outlet and over time.

An important empirical feature uncovered in chapter 3's exploration of the media's coverage of the Court's merits decisions is that the media tends to over-report certain cases, providing saturated coverage of these issue areas. We note that this likely has implications both for the public's understanding of the Court's role in the political system and its perception of the Court as an institution. In chapter 4 we examine this feature in greater detail by analyzing the media's coverage of so-called landmark decisions. Here, we compare the media's attention to these rare cases with its coverage of those cases that history has not identified as particularly salient. We then turn to more detailed substantive discussions of those landmark and non-landmark cases that serve to generate greater amounts of media attention.

Chapter 5 focuses on the media's reporting on the personalities present in the Court. It is often clear that the media treat the work of the Court as an afterthought when compared to any or all other news about the personalities on the Court. A confirmation, resignation, retirement, or death of a justice completely eclipses reporting about the orders and opinions of the justices, suggesting that the individual justice or nominee is much more critical at the beginning and end of a career than while serving on the Bench. In this chapter we explore the nature of the coverage of Justices Blackmun and Stevens over the course of their tenures on the High Bench, paying particular attention to those events that are associated with spikes in coverage of them.

In chapter 6 we take stock of our findings and speculate on the new myth's effect on the Court's institutional credibility. As we noted in chapter 5, justices are more newsworthy as they take their seat and as they leave. Between these moments, the justices and the great bulk of their work do not fit the imperatives of the news media. This is not to say that the media does not cover the Court and the justices. Instead, the media filters the work of the Court in order to achieve "newsworthiness" (or to attract an audience) more so than it does the other branches of government. The filters the media employ are similar to those used with the other branches of government—for example, concentration on stories that involve conflict and interpretation that focuses on who gains or loses electorally; thus the media is constantly putting the square peg of the Supreme Court into the round hole of the normal media routine. As a result, the complexities of cases are ignored or misunderstood. The news cycle demands that cases be reported when they are decided; the actual decision, after all, is the trigger that brings the media's attention to the Court. The import of a decision and its implications on policy and law, however, oftentimes cannot be fully understood without the fullness of some time. Still, the media must report the win or the loss. Victories and defeats are similar to the horse race coverage of politics. Who is ahead? Who is behind? How does a given outcome advantage one political group or another? The media understand this type of story very well indeed, and therefore it is their default approach to coverage. As a result the analysis of the implications of a ruling—the real consequences of a decision—are often left unexplored. The media has no time for them; they need the body count. The public, therefore, is presented with a warped portrayal of the true work of the Court. Can the public's judgments of the Court be valid? Perhaps more importantly, given the Court's unique position and role in our pluralistic political system, to what extent does the nature of the media's coverage of the Court bear upon the public's support for it? We take up these questions in our concluding chapter.

Notes

1 Obviously, this "myth" is largely an empirical fiction (see, for example, Segal and Spaeth 2002). Yet, it is operative among a substantial proportion of the elite public (Scheb and Lyons 2000), and its prevalence appears to act as a "shield" in those instances when the Court's outputs are cast in more political terms (Baird and Gangl 2006, 606).

2 See, for example, Adam Liptak, "Roberts Makes a Getaway from the Scorn," *New York Times*, July 3, 2012; Thomas Friedman, "Taking One for the Country," *New York Times*, July 1, 2012; Adam Liptak, "Roberts's Delicate Twist," *New York Times*, June 29, 2012.

3 Linda Greenhouse, "Surprising Decision," *New York Times*, June 29, 1992: A1.

4 Adam Liptak, "Roberts's Delicate Twist," *New York Times*, June 29, 2012: A1.

10 Introduction: The Myths of the Court

5 Linda Greenhouse, "Souter Joins Liberals in Florida Case," *New York Times*, January 23, 1991:A16.
6 Adam Liptak, "A Rare Rebuke, in Front of a Nation," *New York Times*, January 29, 2010:A12.
7 Gibson and Caldeira make this point with respect to the confirmation process (2009; see especially chapters 5 and 6).

References

Baird, Vanessa A., and Amy Gangl. 2006. "Shattering the Myth of Legality: The Impact of the Media's Framing of Supreme Court Procedures on Perceptions of Fairness." *Political Psychology* 27 (4):597–614.

Bennett, W. Lance. 1996. "An Introduction to Journalism Norms and Representations of Politics." *Political Communications* 13 (4):373–84.

Boykoff, Maxwell T., and Jules M. Boykoff. 2007. "Climate Change and Journalistic Norms: A Case-Study of U.S. Mass-Media Coverage." *Geoforum* 38 (6):1190–1204.

Caldeira, Gregory A. 1986. "Neither the Purse Nor the Sword: Dynamics of Public Confidence in the Supreme Court." *American Political Science Review* 80:1209–26.

Christenson, Dino P., and David M. Glick. 2014. "Roberts' Health Care Decision Disrobed: The Microfoundations of the Court's Legitimacy." Working paper, Boston University.

Clawson, Rosalee A., Elizabeth R. Kegler, and Eric N. Waltenburg. 2003. "Supreme Court Legitimacy and Group-Centric Forces: Black Support for Capital Punishment and Affirmative Action." *Political Behavior* 25:289–311.

Clawson, Rosalee A., and Eric N. Waltenburg. 2009. *Legacy and Legitimacy: Black Americans and the Supreme Court*. Philadelphia: Temple University Press.

Davis, Richard. 1994. *Decisions and Images: The Supreme Court and the Press*. Englewood Cliffs, NJ: Prentice-Hall.

———. 2005. *Electing Justice: Fixing the Supreme Court Nominating Process*. New York: Oxford University Press.

———. 2011. *Justices and Journalists: The U.S. Supreme Court and the Media*. New York: Cambridge University Press.

Easton, David. 1965. *A Systems Analysis of Political Life*. New York: Wiley.

Entman, Robert M., and David L. Paletz. 1980. "Media and the Conservative Myth." *Journal of Communications* 30 (4):154–65.

Epstein, Lee, and Jack Knight. 1998. *The Choices Justices Make*. Washington, DC: CQ Press.

Fiscus, Ronald J. 1991. "Of Constitutions and Constitutional Interpretation." *Polity* 24 (Winter):313–22.

Franklin, Charles H., and Liane C. Kosaki. 1995. "Media, Knowledge, and Public Evaluations of the Supreme Court." In *Contemplating Courts*, pp. 352–376. ed. L. Epstein. Washington, DC: CQ Press.

Gans, Herbert J. 1979. *Deciding What's News*. New York: Pantheon Books.

Gibson, James L., and Gregory A. Caldeira. 2009. *Citizens, Courts, and Confirmations: Positivity Theory and the Judgments of the American People*. Princeton, NJ: Princeton University Press.

———. 2011. "Has Legal Realism Damaged the Legitimacy of the U.S. Supreme Court?" *Law and Society Review* 45 (1):195–219.

Gibson, James L., Gregory A. Caldeira, and Vanessa A. Baird. 1998. "On the Legitimacy of National High Courts." *American Political Science Review* 92:343–58.

Hall Jamieson, Kathleen, and Paul Waldman. 2003. *The Press Effect: Politicians, Journalists, and the Stories That Shape the Political World*. New York: Oxford University Press.

Johnston, Christopher D., and Brandon L. Bartels. 2010. "Sensationalism and Sobriety: Differential Media Exposure and Attitudes Toward American Courts." *Public Opinion Quarterly* 74 (2):260–86.

O'Brien, David M. 1996. *Storm Center: The Supreme Court in American Politics*. 4th ed. New York: W. W. Norton.

Rowland, Kara. 2010. "Obama Nominates Kagan to High Court." *Washington Times*, May 10. www.washingtontimes.com/news/2010/may/10/obama-appoint-kagan-high-court/?page=all (last accessed January 16, 2012).

Scheb, John M., and William Lyons. 2000. "The Myth of Legality and Public Evaluation of the Supreme Court." *Social Science Quarterly* 81 (4):928–40.

Segal, Jeffrey A., and Harold J. Spaeth. 2002. *The Supreme Court and the Attitudinal Model Revisited*. New York: Cambridge University Press.

Segal, Jeffrey A., Harold J. Spaeth, and Sara C. Benesh. 2005. *The Supreme Court in the American Legal System*. New York: Cambridge University Press.

Soroka, Stuart N. 2012. "The Gatekeeping Function: Distributions of Information in Media and the Real World." *Journal of Politics* 74 (2):514–28.

Spill, Rorie L., and Zoe M. Oxley. 2003. "Philosopher Kings or Political Actors: How the Media Portray the Supreme Court." *Judicature* 87 (1):23–29.

Stevenson, Richard W. 2005. "President Names Roberts as Choice for Chief Justice." *New York Times*, September 5. http://www.nytimes.com/2005/09/05/politics/politicsspecial1/05cnd-scotus.html?pagewanted=all (last accessed January 16, 2012).

2

CONFIRMATION AND THE "CULT OF PERSONALITY"

Of the three national policy making institutions, the Supreme Court is the most removed from the press and public. In no small part, this is a consequence of its constitutional design. Unelected, and serving for terms of "good behavior," its members are intended *not to be held* to any type of direct democratic accountability. But this separation is also the product of the studied behavior of the justices, the norms associated with the Court's operation, and the traditional deference that the institution is afforded. Historically, the justices have been loath to make themselves available to the Fourth Estate or to interact with the mass public. Richard Davis, for example, reports that the willingness of Supreme Court justices (and certainly not all of them even now) to "go public" is a very recent phenomenon (2011, Preface; 2014). And this isolation from the press is imposed on other employees of the Court as well. For example, concerns over press leaks led the Court in 1987 to promulgate a "Code of Conduct for Supreme Court Law Clerks" that included the stipulation that the clerks were permitted to discuss their work for the Court only with the justices and other law clerks (O'Brien 2005, 120).

As a policy making institution in a democracy, the operation of the Supreme Court is far from transparent. Many of its most consequential actions (e.g., deciding what to decide, the conference on the merits of a case, the discussions and compromises over the final scope and shape of the Court's majority opinion) occur out of the view of the press and public. And then there is the effect of the prevailing "myth of legality" with all of its trappings—the raised bench, the marble temple, the priestly garb. This quasi-religious symbolism results in a reverence for the Court that separates it from democratic politics (Davis 2011, 119; Segal, Spaeth, and Benesh 2005). Indeed, the "cult of the robe" makes the press, the public, and other members of the government reluctant to probe into the intimate machinations of the Court or to expose what Davis (2011) refers to as the "human element" of the institution's actors. Simply put, to peer behind the purple curtain, or to peek under the robes of the priests of the law, would be untoward.[1]

These types of strictures, however, do not operate during the confirmation of justices to the Court. Confirmations are decidedly *political and public* events.[2] At no other time are the individual members of the Court thrown as fully into the vortex of democratic politics as they are during the confirmation process. During confirmations, interest groups mount campaigns for and against a nominee; they take out advertisements and offer opposition research to media outlets. Public rallies are not unheard of.[3] Indeed, Davis describes the battle over the Bork nomination in 1987 (an outlying event perhaps) as being closer to a battle for elective office that a traditional appointment to the Court (2011, 95). Meanwhile, Senate examiners, along with asking about precedent and judicial philosophy, feel little compunction about probing a nominee's personal life, his or her qualifications for a seat on the High Bench, or asking for explanations concerning prior beliefs, statements, and behaviors. In the process the nominee is necessarily exposed to public questioning and provides answers for public consumption. During the time period from nomination through confirmation, the nominees and their pasts are placed in a glass house.

Thus, the nature of the confirmation process pierces the insulation the "cult of the robe" affords the Court and the justices, and the human element of the justices is on display. Interestingly, despite the presence of information that is consistent with both the "cult of the robe" and the "cult of personality" in the confirmation process, the press seems to focus on the latter elements, allowing the new myth of the "cult of personality" to take root. In this chapter, we explore the connection between the confirmation process and the emergence of that new myth.

Our exploration of the rise of the "cult of personality" during the confirmation process is organized as follows. We begin in the next section with a brief review of what we know about confirmations to the Supreme Court, paying particular attention to the media's role in that process. In the third section we discuss our data collection and conduct our analyses. We show that Senate hearings on recent nominees to the Court produce greater amounts of information consistent with the "cult of the robe" and to a lesser degree the "cult of personality." Media coverage of these hearings, however, presents a distorted image to the public. Although touching on information that reinforces the legal myth, the media chooses to emphasize the "cult of personality" in what it deems to be newsworthy in the confirmation process.

Research on Supreme Court Confirmations

Confirmation to the Supreme Court has long been a subject of significant interest to judicial scholars. And as a result, we have a good understanding of the primary

14 Confirmation and the "Cult of Personality"

forces affecting that process. Ideology and partisanship are two of the most significant of these forces (Epstein and Segal 2007; Segal, Cameron, and Cover 1992; Segal and Spaeth 2002). Presidents seek to nominate individuals who are confirmable and who hold views similar to their own.[4] Individual senators likewise are mindful of a nominee's ideological position relative to their own preferences as well as the preferences of their constituents. Thus, the individual senator is more likely to vote to confirm a nominee the closer that nominee is to those ideological positions.

That ideology and partisanship are so prominent in the confirmation process is, perhaps, not surprising. After all, these forces are well established as affecting the decisional outputs of both the legislative and executive branches (Poole and Rosenthal 1991; Weisberg 1978). But of greater consequences to our purposes here is that it is not unusual for the operation of these forces to provoke political conflicts between presidents and the Senate (Bond and Fleisher 2000; McCormick and Wittkopf 1990). There are great stakes in making appointments to the judiciary. And this has been recognized since the earliest days of the Constitution's operation. For example, following their stinging defeat at the hands of the Jeffersonian-Republicans in the election of 1800, the Federalists responded with the *Judiciary Act of 1801*, creating a number of judicial vacancies. The partisan politics of the Act were obvious. Even Federalist Senator Gouverneur Morris quipped to a friend: "About to experience a heavy gale of adverse wind; can they [the Federalists] be blamed for casting many anchors to hold their ship through the storm?" (qtd. in Glickstein 2012, 544)

Presidential legacies can be extended, and so during confirmation hearings both the legislative and executive branches vie over the shape of the federal bench. Given these stakes, political gamesmanship is almost guaranteed. Indeed, confirmations oftentimes are catalysts for the inter-branch conflicts that are essentially built into the Constitution's design.

Along with the "Midnight Appointments," other examples of inter-branch conflict are plentiful. During Reconstruction, the Radical Republicans reduced the number of seats on the Supreme Court from 10 to 7 rather than permit Andrew Johnson to nominate a Supreme Court justice. In the more contemporary era, there is the failed attempt of Lyndon Johnson (a self-made "lame duck" mired in an increasingly unpopular war) to elevate his friend Abe Fortas to chief justice; Nixon's two failed attempts to pursue a "Southern strategy"; the controversy over William Rehnquist's initial appointment as an associate justice and then his elevation to chief; the fiasco of the Bork nomination during the Reagan administration; and the spectacle of the Thomas nomination during the first Bush administration after the allegations of sexual harassment were made public.

Historically, strong qualifications have helped to pave the way for smooth confirmations (Epstein et al. 2006; Segal, Cameron, and Cover 1992). Well-qualified nominees through the Clinton administration garnered few "no" votes. Impeccable qualifications could even militate against expected opposition in a Senate that might be predisposed, by dint of partisanship and ideological preference, to oppose a president's nominee. Despite his well-documented conservative philosophy, for example, President Reagan's nomination of the highly qualified Antonin Scalia was confirmed by a vote of 98 to 0. This tendency, however, seems to be coming to an end, as the number of negative votes is increasing seemingly without regard to the qualifications of the nominee.[5] By the administration of George W. Bush, substantial numbers of negative votes became the norm, and a new metric—weighted by the incidence of "nay" votes—for the evaluation of the opposition to any Court nominee came into existence. John Roberts, for example, received 22 negative votes; yet, there is consensus that his nomination was a relatively smooth one.

Although the expectation is that the president's nominee ultimately will secure confirmation, the margin of the vote in support is not certain. And this uncertainty attracts media attention (Watson and Stookey 1988). That there will be votes in opposition means a political battle may be in the offing, with the consequences that the story now fits easily within the media's preference for "horse race" coverage. Winners, losers, political strategies, the expenditure of political capital—themes with which the media are especially comfortable—can be brought to bear in the coverage of a confirmation. Amplifying the media's penchant to portray a confirmation as an event over which a political battle likely looms is the tendency of presidents to "go public" and appeal to the voters that their "candidate is well suited for the position and that only the partisan, ideological Senate can stand in the way" (Epstein and Segal 2007, 78). In other words, the actions of a president almost preordain the confirmation to be interpreted as a political fight between the branches. And finally, interest groups mobilize in response to a confirmation, again creating a climate of political conflict. Interest groups lobby for and against nominees using advertising campaigns, talk radio, YouTube clips, and social networking sites. These campaigns are not lost on the media, and they become compelling narratives in this era of "infotainment."

It is our contention that the nature of the contemporary confirmation process plays into the media's emphasis on the personal, the sensational, and the controversial. Coverage of these characteristics eclipses coverage of the substantive content of the nomination and confirmation process. This contention, of course, is subject to empirical testing, and to that end, we analyze the four most recent confirmation hearings to assess the nature of the questions and responses during each nominee's testimony as well as the behavior of the members of the Judiciary Committee. We then compare the content of the testimony before the Judiciary Committee to the media's coverage of that same testimony. We find that the media does report a fair amount of the actual content of the hearings. Nevertheless, the news consumer is treated to a skewed image—one emphasizing personalities and certain issues.

16 Confirmation and the "Cult of Personality"

The Data[6]

Supreme Court confirmations are high-profile events that introduce the new justice to the country and provide a forum for members of the Judiciary Committee to take appropriate positions (Mayhew 1974). Even uncontroversial hearings last several days. The media cover these events, though not from opening gavel to closing. Again, we contend that the questions and answers that make their way to the pages and airwaves are not randomly selected (see Soroka 2012). Rather, some questions and some senators are much more likely to make the cut. This systematic culling of content, then, suggests to the public that either the Court is a one-trick pony or that the members of the Senate Judiciary Committee are concerned only with a handful of issues. To evaluate the verisimilitude between the hearings and the media coverage, we gathered transcripts of the four most recent Supreme Court confirmation hearings—Chief Justice Roberts, and Justices Alito, Sotomayor, and Kagan. Conveniently, we have two justices nominated by a Republican president (George W. Bush) and two by a Democratic president (Barack Obama). Similarly, during the 109th Congress, the Congress in session during the Roberts and Alito hearings, the Republicans held a slight majority (55–45) in the Senate, while the Democrats held a similar advantage (57–43) in the 111th Congress, the Congress that confirmed Sotomayor and Kagan. In all instances, then, the president and the Senate majority were of the same party, providing a modicum of natural controls over the variability of coverage due to political context.

For each transcript, we coded each time a senator spoke (n = 3,696). Each instance was coded for up to three substantive areas. Additionally, we coded for the identity of the speaker; whether the utterance was a question or a statement, an opening remark, a follow-up question, or a request for clarification; and whether the nominee offered a response. We also coded whether the question or remark was positive, negative, or neutral, and if the statement or question was an endorsement of the nominee. Finally, following Watson and Stookey (1995), we coded if the senator was acting as a *Partisan, Advertiser, Advocate*, or *Evaluator*.[7]

To assess media coverage, we collected all news stories reporting on the hearings from the day each hearing opened through the day after the hearings closed from the *New York Times*, the *Washington Post*, and *USA Today* newspapers, and ABC, CBS, and NBC television news (n = 346). Using these outlets, we obtain a good sample of national coverage. We then coded up to eight mentions of issues for the reporter, the nominee, and senators in the order mentioned. We also recorded whether the nominee was referred to as a "judge" or "justice" in the first mention; whether party distinctions were drawn; whether the story predicted the outcome of the confirmation; whether conflict between senators or between senators and the nominee was mentioned; and any mention of other relevant players (e.g., President Bush, Chief Justice Rehnquist, President Reagan, or the nominee's spouse). Finally, we coded how long (in terms of the number of sentences) each story was.

We created two separate datasets to analyze the content of the hearings vis-à-vis their coverage in the media. In both datasets we collapsed detailed substantive content categories into broader groupings. Our broader categories include Judicial Philosophy (or the "Cult of the Robe"), Qualifications, Press Characterization of the Hearing, "Cult of Personality," Abortion, Federal Power, Discrimination, and Procedure. For example, the *Qualifications* category includes, among other things, any mention or question of previous judicial experience, judicial temperament, or arguments before the Supreme Court. The "*Cult of Personality*" category includes references to the nominee's background or family, paper trail concerns, and references to other justices (e.g., John Roberts's service as a clerk to William Rehnquist). *Judicial Philosophy* (the "Cult of the Robe") includes mentions of respect for precedent, comments about the Constitution or judicial activism, the role of the chief justice, and various approaches to interpreting constitutional or statutory intent. Using these broader categories, we were better able to compare content across hearings as well as to identify content that was unique to each hearing—for example, the baseball analogy or reference to Hurricane Katrina in the Roberts hearing, discussions of CAP ("Concerned Alumni of Princeton") in the Alito hearing, Sotomayor addressing her "wise Latina" comment, and Kagan's work at Harvard. We now turn to our analyses of these rich datasets.

"Look Who's Talking!"

We begin our analysis by taking soundings on our data of the four most recent confirmation hearings to produce a sense of the landscape of the modern Senate confirmation process. To a large degree our findings regarding the activity of the senators are consistent with prior studies of confirmation and legislative behavior. The leadership of the Judiciary Committee does indeed "lead" by taking up more time at the microphone, and in homage to the fading norms of the Congress, senior members of the Committee are heard more frequently than their more junior counterparts. (Both relationships are significant at $p \leq .10$, just missing conventional levels of statistical security.)

Of course, partisanship is a near constant in congressional behavior, and not surprisingly, it is present in the four confirmation hearings under examination here. Senators belonging to the party opposite that of the president spoke more often, and their remarks or questions were more likely to be negative than neutral or positive in tone.[8] The relationship is highly significant and attains a reasonably strong measure of association ($p \leq .00; V = .38$). Furthermore, the underlying behavior (viz., more incredulous examiners posing challenging questions) is not unique to the partisan confirmation process. It is reminiscent, for example, of

18 Confirmation and the "Cult of Personality"

content analyses of Supreme Court oral arguments. Empirical tests have shown that the justices tend to question more vigorously the side against which they are leaning (Epstein, Landes, and Posner 2010). In the end, however, it is important to recognize that the senators' questions and commentary during the hearings were overwhelming neutral. Nearly two-thirds of the statements contained neither sting nor stroke.

That these confirmation hearings did not appear to occasion particularly extreme positions among the senators is striking, given the magnitude of polarization that that has come to characterize the present-day Congress (see, for example, McCarty, Poole, and Rosenthal 2006; Sinclair 2006)[9] and the tendency of the Judiciary Committee to attract more ideologically zealous members (Smith and Deering 1997). A possible explanation is the mediating effect of the "cult of the robe." As Watson and Stookey note, the perceived legitimate lines of inquiry constrain the nature and reach of the senators' partisan questions and statements (1995, 152–53). Thus, it might be that in the absence of controversial nominations (as was the case here) both ideologues and extreme partisans are less likely to pursue dogmatic lines of inquiry. As a result, not only were loaded statements and questions rare, senators playing the role of the Partisan largely did so alone. Only 5.2% of the time did senators adopt a partisan role in their statements about, or questions put to, the nominee. Their choice already made, these Partisans used the "hearings to secure or defeat the nomination" (Watson and Stookey 1995, 152).

Rather than the role of Partisan, we find that in their statements and questions, most senators take on the role of the Evaluator (41.2%), portraying themselves as weighing the evidence necessary to make a wise choice, or the Advocate (47.7%), seeking to advertise or educate through their participation. For example, on the first day of the Roberts hearings Senator Arlen Specter was clearly playing the role of Evaluator, noting, "I have reserved my own judgment on your nomination until the hearings are concluded . . ."[10]

If we explore the Advocate role in greater detail, we see it is more heavily weighted toward the role of an "Advertiser," a widely recognized and expected mode of congressional behavior (Mayhew 1974). And this makes good sense. Senators are well aware that confirmation hearings in the television age afford them the opportunity to show their fealty to and support for issues of particular importance to their constituents. Guaranteed to appear on C-SPAN, with luck these statements will also appear on the nightly news or in the pages of the hometown paper. Senator Kennedy provides a typical example of this role when he took the opportunity during the second day of the Alito hearings to advertise his position on both personal privacy and executive power:

> In an era where the White House is abusing power, is excusing and authorizing torture and is spying on American citizens, I find Judge Alito's support for an all-powerful executive branch to be genuinely troubling.

Under the president's spying program, there are no checks and balances. There is no outside review of the legality of this brazen infringement on the civil rights and liberties of the American people. Undeterred by the public outcry, the president vows to continue spying on American citizens.

Finally, the Validator, the last of Watson and Stookey's roles, appears only 5.9% of the time in the senators' comments and questions. Again, from the Alito hearings, we have Senator Hatch discussing the controversy over Alito's lack of initial recusal in a case where he had a financial interest.[11] He essentially allows Alito to tell his side of the story and then asks:

Hatch: In other words, there was never any possibility of your benefitting financially, no matter how that case came out, is that right?

Alito: There was absolutely no chance and . . .

Hatch: You actually did recuse yourself when the question was eventually raised, even though you didn't have to?

Alito: That's correct, Senator.

Hatch: Did you genuinely feel you were either legally or ethically required to recuse under those circumstances?

Alito: I did not think the code required me . . .

Hatch: You were just going beyond, which has been your philosophy . . .

When the confirmation hearings are examined separately, these general trends are largely maintained. Yet, there are some noteworthy exceptions. For example, in Samuel Alito's confirmation hearings, the Partisan role is relatively prominent. Fully 10% of the time senators adopted this role when posing questions to or making statements about Alito. By way of contrast, the Partisan role appears only 4.6% of the time in the confirmation hearings of John Roberts. Significantly, this is the second-highest rate of occurrence for this role. The Sotomayor and Kagan hearings are notable for their relative absence of partisanship. The Partisan role appears in the senators' statements and questions directed at Sonia Sotomayor merely 2.7% of the time, and it occurs only 1.9% of the time in Elena Kagan's hearings.

Closer examination of the senators adopting the Partisan role indicates that this is largely a GOP phenomenon. Republicans accounted for 142 of the 191 (74%) instances of Partisan role behavior in the confirmation hearings ($\chi^2 = 56.71$, $p \leq .00$). To be sure, the overwhelming proportion of these Partisan questions or statements was in support of a nominee of their president's party; this is largely the nature of the Partisan role behavior among Democratic senators. But Republicans were also far more willing to step into the role of partisan opponent, using the confirmation hearings to challenge a Democratic president's choice of Court nominee. Republicans adopted the Partisan role 48.2% and 69.2% of the time in the Sotomayor and Kagan hearings respectively. Democrats, on the other hand,

20 Confirmation and the "Cult of Personality"

played the partisan "attack-dog" just 11.9% and 23.9% of the time in the Roberts and Alito hearings. As a result, the proportion of Republican Partisan role behavior in the Sotomayor and Kagan hearings is statistically the same as the Partisan role behavior among Democrats ($|z| = 1.27, p \leq .20$), as senators from either side of the aisle spoke out either to challenge or to defend the Democratic nominees. The proportion of Democratic Partisan role behavior in the Roberts and Alito hearings, however, is significantly different (smaller) than the Partisan role behavior of the Republicans ($|z| = 10.8, p \leq .00$). To put it simply, the Democrats did not wage partisan attacks on Roberts and Alito; as a result, they left the field to these nominees' partisan defenders.

There is also some evidence across the hearings of a "gender effect" in the nature and tone of the questions and statements. In the case of both Sotomayor and Kagan, nearly 90% of the senators' questions and comments were neutral in tone, while neutral questions and comments occurred well under 50% of the time in the Roberts and Alito hearings ($\chi^2 = 804.7, p \leq .00$). Perhaps the senators walked softly, avoiding pointed questions and comments rather than risk offending female constituents.[12]

Finally, the Sotomayor hearings, in particular, exhibited a very different distribution of roles among the senators. Where the other three hearings witnessed the senators adopting the Advocate role at least 50% of the time, in the Sotomayor hearing, the senators overwhelming played the role of Evaluator (78%). According to Watson and Stookey, Evaluators are "unsettled or uncertain about the nominee on some particular issue that involves the senator's core requirements for a Supreme Court justice" and use their questions to resolve this uncertainty (1995, 150). Significantly, both Democratic and Republican senators adopted the Evaluator role well over 50% of the time, and this seems to be the result of questions about the standards Sotomayor would employ in her decisional behavior if elevated to the Court. More than a month prior to her confirmation hearings, Sotomayor's "wise Latina" statement attracted public attention. That statement, coupled with President Obama's declaration that he would seek to nominate "empathetic justices," likely engendered concerns among the senators over the judicial philosophy that Sotomayor would bring to the High Bench. Consequently, senators adopted the Evaluator role and used the hearings to probe Sotomayor's approach to judging.

"Let's Give Them Something to Talk About!"

Turning to the substantive content of the hearings, we limit our analysis to those substantive categories that accounted for at least 5% of all the mentions we coded in the hearings. Their relative magnitude is displayed in Figure 2.1. Of those categories that meet this criterion, we find that senators continue to support and perpetuate the "cult of the robe." Overall, the questions and comments regarding judicial philosophy were the modal category, accounting for about one-fifth of

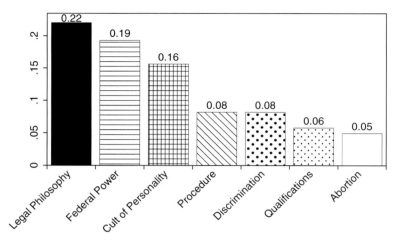

FIGURE 2.1 Categories Accounting for at Least Five Percent of the Mentions in Confirmation Hearings

all the mentions, and outdistancing the "cult of personality" by about 6%. Sandwiched between the two "cults" are statements and questions focusing on the scope of federal power (19%). About 8% of the time, the senators were referring to the hearing itself or its procedures when they spoke. This percentage is about equal to the share of comments and inquiries covering the issue of discrimination, broadly defined.[13] Concerns or compliments regarding a nominee's qualifications and the issue of abortion are the only other issues that garner enough attention to reach the 5% threshold (see Figure 2.1). Otherwise, the hearings ranged across a large number of topics from the *False Claims Act* to the EPA, from seatbelts to Ponzi schemes and even favorite movies.[14] Clearly, many issues addressed in the hearings essentially were idiosyncratic to specific senators, that is peripheral rather than salient to the full body.

Not surprisingly, given the norms of the Senate, neither party dominated the floor. Across all four hearings, the percentages are about equal, with Democrats commenting or questioning about 52% of the time and the GOP holding close at 48%. All the same, there are notable differences between the parties in the nature or focus of the questions and comments. Republicans emphasized the categories of Legal Philosophy (the "cult of the robe") and Abortion, in each case outpacing their Democratic counterparts by about a 3-to-2 clip. Democrats, meanwhile, focused more on the nominees' personal stories (the "cult of personality") and were more concerned with the procedures of the confirmation process, overtaking their Republican counterparts at roughly the same levels by which they were surpassed in the categories of Republican emphasis (see Figure 2.2). For example, in his opening statements for the hearings of Chief Justice Roberts, Senator Leahy

22 Confirmation and the "Cult of Personality"

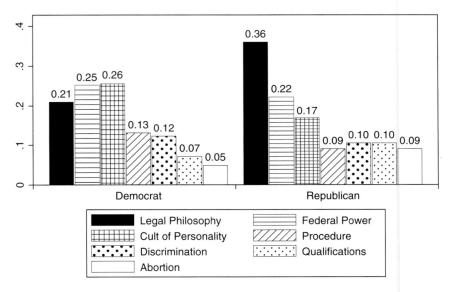

FIGURE 2.2 Categories Accounting for at Least Five Percent of the Mentions in Confirmation Hearings by Party

noted, "A few days ago, William Rehnquist passed away.... I know, Judge Roberts, that was a particularly difficult time for you because of your close relationship with him."

Additional party differences worthy of note come into focus when we examine the GOP-led hearings versus the hearings where the Democrats were in control of the Judiciary Committee. First, it is clear that procedure is of substantive concern when you are running the show and your party's nominee is in the spotlight. Along this vein, senators support nominees of a same-party president by pontificating about the qualifications of the president's choice. For example, in his introduction of Sonia Sotomayor, Senator Leahy said:

> Judge Sotomayor's qualifications are outstanding. She's had more federal court judicial experience than any nominee to the United States Supreme Court in nearly a hundred years. She is the first nominee in well over a century to be nominated to three different federal judgeships by three different presidents.... I hope all America is encouraged by Judge Sotomayor's achievements and by her nomination to the nation's highest court. Hers is a success story in which all—all—Americans can take pride."

The GOP dominated the qualifications conversation during the Roberts and Alito hearings (68.4% and 88.9%, respectively); yet, they elided this topic during the Sotomayor and Kagan hearings—in both cases accounting for just over one-third of the mentions dealing with qualifications. One way to interpret these distributions is that discussions of qualifications and procedures operate as defensive topics to parry attacks from the opposition.

We see many of these trends replicated when we disaggregate the hearings data and turn our attention to the individual confirmations. Accordingly, five of the seven substantive categories discussed above meet a 5% criterion across all four hearings; only abortion and qualifications miss the cut. Moreover, the top three categories remain the top three categories in three of the four hearings, albeit with some shuffling. Federal power is the modal category in both Republican hearings (Kennedy to Alito: "You argued that the attorney general should have the absolute immunity, even for actions that he knows to be unlawful or unconstitutional . . ."). It drops to second place, however, in the Kagan hearings and falls to third in the Sotomayor confirmation. The "cult of the robe" makes a strong showing across all four hearings. It is the modal category for both Sotomayor and Kagan, and it is a close second in the Roberts hearings. It is the third most frequently occurring category in the Alito hearings, replaced as "runner up" by the "cult of personality." Indeed, the "cult of personality" has its strongest absolute showing in the Alito confirmation, but it ranks second for Sotomayor as well and attains third-place status for Kagan. Take, for example, Senator Biden's questioning of Alito:

> Biden: ". . . but I did ask you when you were kind enough to come to my office about Concerned Alumni of Princeton. Were you aware of some of the other things they were saying that had nothing to do with ROTC? Because there was a great deal of controversy."

Only in the case of the Roberts hearings does this category fail to rank in the top three; it falls to fourth place, tied with procedures, in his confirmation.

Perhaps the most interesting difference to emerge when examining the individual hearings data is seen in the Sotomayor confirmation. While judicial philosophy, or the "cult of the robe," was discussed frequently during all four confirmations, it attains its greatest magnitude during the questioning of Judge Sonia Sotomayor. As we have already noted, the widespread attention given to Sotomayor and her "wise Latina" statement likely led to more senators remaining on the fence regarding her confirmation (playing the role of Evaluator). This phrase also necessitated that the senators use their allotted time to discuss and delve into Sotomayor's judicial philosophy, as Senator Sessions did: "Let me recall that yesterday you said it's simple fidelity to the law. . . . I heartily agree with that. However, you previously have said that the court of appeals is where policy is made." Consequently, the judicial philosophy category took up over 30% of the total conversation during her four days before the Judiciary Committee (see Figures 2.3–2.6).

24 Confirmation and the "Cult of Personality"

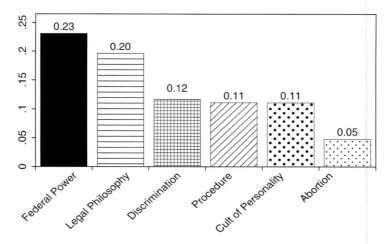

FIGURE 2.3 Distribution of Categories for Roberts Hearings

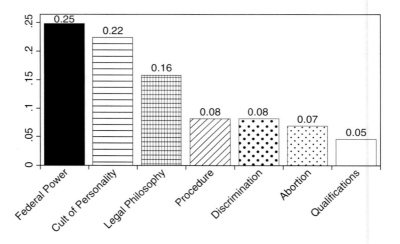

FIGURE 2.4 Distribution of Categories for Alito Hearings

In sum these four hearings are notable for their overwhelmingly neutral tone (or at least lack of extensive partisanship); the appearance of the "cult of the robe" and, to a lesser degree (and somewhat surprisingly), the "cult of personality" in the senators' questions and comments; the infrequent appearance of most substantive issue areas; and the committee leadership's domination of the microphone. In other words, the hearings concentrated on phenomena that are fundamentally concerned with a nominee's anticipated judicial role and behavior

Confirmation and the "Cult of Personality" 25

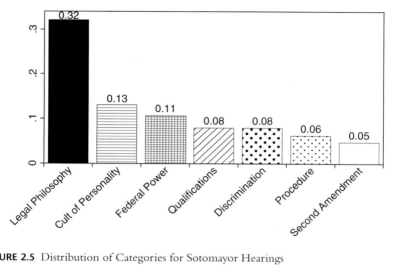

FIGURE 2.5 Distribution of Categories for Sotomayor Hearings

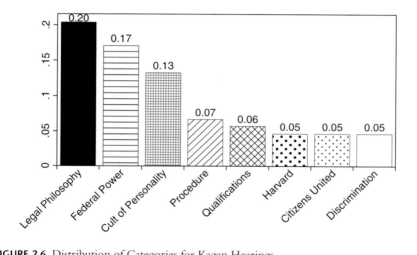

FIGURE 2.6 Distribution of Categories for Kagan Hearings

and follow established Senate procedural rules and expected decorum. There was neither high drama nor partisan fireworks.[15] But how did the media portray these hearings? It is to that question that we now turn.

Look Who They Talked About

The lens the media uses is quite focused when mentioning the senators on the Judiciary Committee. For the most part the leadership dominates the coverage.

26 Confirmation and the "Cult of Personality"

Three of the most mentioned senators held Committee leadership positions for most of the hearings. Breaking the hearings down by the party of the nominating president much stays the same. Using a 5% threshold of all comments made to narrow and better focus our analysis, two additional Republicans (Senators Kyl and Cornyn) make the grade in the two Democratic hearings, and this is to be expected, given the more frequent participation of opposition senators. A similar pattern appears in the GOP hearings, where Senators Biden and Feingold achieve the 5% threshold. It is important to note, however, that in absolute terms no single senator is mentioned very often. Senator Patrick Leahy, for example, was a member of the Committee leadership, either as ranking minority member or chair, for all four hearings, and made print or air fewer than 80 times. Considering that this number is the sum of mentions in six media sources, covering four confirmations that lasted a total of 15 days, this is a very small number indeed.

There are four exceptions to the media's focus on the Committee leadership. Senators Graham, Kennedy, Schumer, and Feinstein garner more or almost as much attention as the leadership across the hearings. The attention paid to Graham is likely due to his unique status as a Republican member of the Judiciary Committee indicating support for an Obama nominee. Or perhaps it was due to his soft Southern drawl, peppered with colorful terms and phrases. Regardless, as Robert Barnes and Paul Kane wrote for the *Washington Post*:

> Perhaps it is because Senator Lindsey O. Graham is the only Republican on the Senate Judiciary Committee who said openly that he was considering supporting Judge Sonia Sotomayor. Perhaps it is because he said only a "meltdown" could stand between her and a seat on the Supreme Court. Perhaps it is because he said some of the speeches she had given "bugged the hell out of me." But whenever the South Carolinian spoke during Sotomayor's . . . confirmation hearing, senators stopped fiddling with notes . . . and instead closely watched and listened.[16]

And it was not just the senators. Journalists did too. Senator Kennedy's reputation and longevity on the Judiciary Committee is well established, and it is not surprising that the media would allude to his participation. Additionally, Kennedy's prominent role in the defeat of Robert Bork during the Reagan administration is often discussed anew with each subsequent Republican nomination to the Supreme Court. Both Senators Schumer and Feinstein represent two of the media centers of the nation (New York and California, respectively), and Feinstein had long served as the lone woman on the Committee.[17]

These four exceptions indicate that the identity and prominence of individual senators is a major ingredient in the media's choice of whom to cover. To put it simply, these four senators attracted elevated media attention because of their unique status and the politics this status brought to bear on the confirmation process—Kennedy, the liberal lion in winter; Feinstein, the lone woman on a Committee charged with reviewing the constitutional sensibilities of a person who would occupy a position with the power to affect women's fundamental rights; and Graham, the potential Republican apostate. In other words, the "cult of personality" casts a long and deep shadow over the media's attention to the confirmation process.[18]

What They Talked About

First, a word or two is in order about the structure of media reports on the hearings in order to understand the nature of the information the media conveys about the content of the confirmation process. In essence news stories contain three major and separate types of information. There is the frame and information provided by the reporter, attributions to or quotes from senators, and attributions to or quotes from the nominee. Of these three different types, the reporter-led information substantially outnumbers the other two.[19] Accordingly, if one considers the full "story" as a packet of information provided to the consumer of the news, then the bulk of that information packet is framed and structured by the journalist. Figures 2.7 through 2.9 display the distributions for each "component" of a confirmation story.

Turning first to the media's coverage of the senators' statements and questions during the confirmation hearings, our content analysis indicates that the media does a reasonable job of reporting on senatorial behavior vis-à-vis the substantive issues of interest. Recall, senators focused on the issues of judicial philosophy (the "cult of the robe"), federal power, and the "cult of personality" in that order.

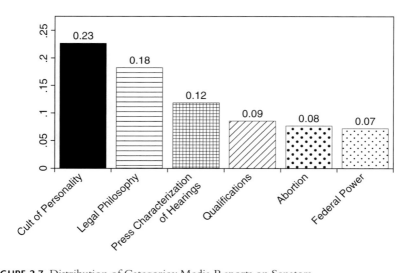

FIGURE 2.7 Distribution of Categories: Media Reports on Senators

28 Confirmation and the "Cult of Personality"

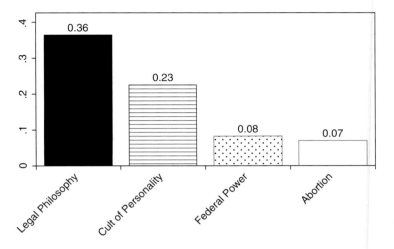

FIGURE 2.8 Distribution of Categories: Media Reports on Nominees

The media got two out of three correct, concentrating on the "cult of personality" (22.7%) and the "cult of the robe" (18.2%). Federal powers, however, reached only sixth place in terms of the frequency of media mentions, accounting for only about 7% of the media's coverage of senatorial questions and remarks. Only two other substantive issue categories clear the 5% criterion that we have applied throughout—qualifications (8.6%) and abortion (7.7%). A new category appears in the media's coverage of the senators—"press characterization of the hearings." It seems that rather than attributing substantive issues to the senators, the reporters used the senators to characterize the hearings. For example, Senator Diane Feinstein was quoted as saying, "She [Sotomayor] has not used catchy phrases. She has answered the questions directly as best she could."[20] This type of attribution occurred 11.9% of the time (see Figure 2.7).

When it comes to reporting the nominees' statements, the coverage is overwhelmingly centered on the "cult of the robe." Over one-third of the nominees' comments and answers can be classified as belonging to this category. The "cult of personality" does make a strong showing in this distribution as well, however (22.6%). And this should not be terribly surprising given the nature of the modern confirmation process as we discussed in chapter 1 (see Figure 2.8).

Of course, inasmuch as the reporter-led issues dominate a story "packet," the comparison between these and the actual hearings are of greatest analytical value. And it is here that we see the most striking differences. Figure 2.9 displays the distribution of the categories for the reporter-led issues, while Table 2.1 reports the proportion of each category in the hearings and the reporter-led issues, as well as significance tests for the differences. Whereas the senators were deeply concerned with judicial philosophy or the "cult of the robe," this occupied the reporters' attention only 12% of the time. Instead, the reporters zeroed in on the "cult of personality," devoting over one-quarter of their sentences to this issue area. For example, Pete Williams, reporting for NBC on the Kagan hearings, noted that "she displayed flashes of humor, especially in response to some unfocused questions." Then the story shows an exchange between Senator Graham and Ms. Kagan:

Graham: No, I just asked you where you were at on Christmas.
Kagan: You know, like all Jews, I was probably at a Chinese restaurant.

Or from NBC's Kelly O'Donnell: "From abortion rights to immigration, they found various ways to call her a liberal." Or from the *Washington Post*'s Robert Barnes and Amy Goldstein: "Sotomayor carefully wrote down each question on

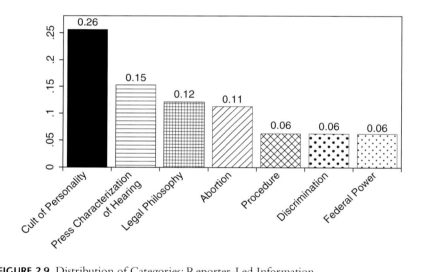

FIGURE 2.9 Distribution of Categories: Reporter-Led Information

TABLE 2.1 Substantive Coverage, Proportion of Categories: Hearings vs. Media Reports

Substantive Category	Hearings	Media	|Difference|	p ≤
Cult of Personality	.16	.26	.10	.00
Cult of the Robe	.22	.12	.10	.00
Abortion	.05	.11	.06	.00
Procedure	.08	.06	.02	.02
Discrimination	.08	.06	.02	.02
Federal Power	.19	.07	.12	.00
Press Characterization	n/a	.15	n/a	n/a

30 Confirmation and the "Cult of Personality"

a legal pad and was circumspect and cautious. Kagan was a bit looser . . . she showed fatigue only once."[21] The differences are highly significant. The reporters also spent a good amount of time characterizing the hearings (15.3%) as well as discussing the hearings' procedural norms or oddities (6.5%).

But the disconnect between the journalists' issue foci and the reality of what transpired in the hearings does not end there. The reporters continued to veer off-course in their discussion (or more accurately, the lack thereof) of additional issues. Accordingly, the amount of attention the senators paid to federal powers was substantial and to be expected, given the expansion of presidential authority with the "war on terror," GOP concerns over activist judges and states' rights,[22] as well as the general curbing of congressional power that reached its zenith during the Rehnquist Court and largely continues in the Roberts Court. Yet, reporters eschewed these issue areas, reporting upon them only 6% of the time. Instead, a greater amount of print space and airtime were devoted to the more provocative and controversial social issues of discrimination and, especially, abortion. Journalistic coverage of discrimination is actually quite close to the actual level of interest exhibited during the hearings (6.2% versus 8.3%). However, reporters devoted a significantly greater amount of attention to abortion than did the senators ($|z| = 7.9, p \leq .00$). Indeed, reporters spent about as much time discussing abortion questions and comments as they did judicial philosophy (11.3% versus 12%). Given that abortion just made the 5% criterion for the hearings (4.9%), it is clear that this particularly controversial issue reaps considerably more attention from reporters than from senators and nominees:

> Senator Orrin G. Hatch (Utah) pressed her [Kagan] on a memo she wrote as a domestic policy aide to President Bill Clinton that said it would be a "disaster" if the American College of Obstetricians and Gynecologists released a finding that the procedure critics call partial-birth abortion was not the only option for preserving a women's life or health.[23]

Examining individual hearings with respect to reporter-led issues reveals that the overemphasis on abortion is an attribute of the Republican hearings and coverage. The most print space and airtime concerning abortion occurred during the Roberts hearings—a full 20% of the attention. No other topic comes close to this amount of scrutiny, and it is well out of proportion to the attention given it in the actual hearings. During his testimony, barely 5% of the discussion touched on abortion. Conversely, nearly one-quarter of that conversation investigated issues related to federal power, whereas reporters gave those issues a mere fraction of their attention (5.9%). Similarly, federal power edged out the "cult of personality" during the Alito hearings (24.8% versus 22.3%) with abortion and discrimination falling substantially farther back (7.5% and 6.9%, respectively). Yet, coverage of his hearings was heavily tipped toward the "cult of personality" and abortion. In particular, the "cult of personality" was included in just over 30% of the coverage.

Confirmation and the "Cult of Personality" 31

Abortion follows as the next most reporter-mentioned issue at 15%. And finally federal power—an issue clearly of concern to the senators at this hearing—was provided more space than during the Roberts hearings, but the meager 12% coverage pales in comparison to the reality of the hearings (see Figures 2.10 and 2.11).

Within the Sotomayor hearings, abortion and discrimination are the only political issues to attain 5% of the media's attention, and just barely so (5.9% and 4.8%, respectively). The coverage of the Kagan hearings is notable for the absence of media attention to political issues.

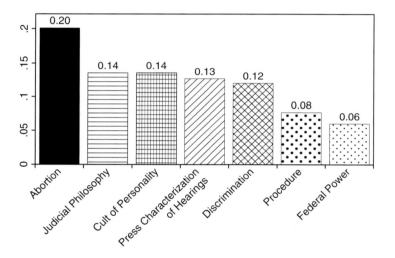

FIGURE 2.10 Distribution of Categories: Media Coverage of Roberts Hearings

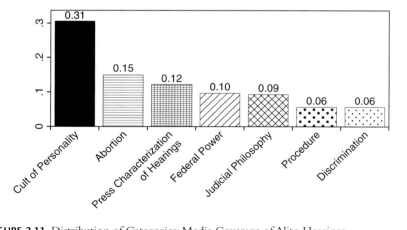

FIGURE 2.11 Distribution of Categories: Media Coverage of Alito Hearings

32 Confirmation and the "Cult of Personality"

In terms of our "cults" of interest, in the Roberts reporter-led coverage, the appearance of the "cult of the robe" and the "cult of personality" are about equal and come second only to mentions of abortion. For the other three nominees, the "cult of personality" is the leading category by substantial amounts and consistently maintains a 2-to-1 advantage over the "cult of the robe." It bears noting that the "cult of the robe" encompassed a greater amount of discussion and questions than the "cult of personality" in every confirmation but Samuel Alito's; in Sonia Sotomayor's hearings, references to the "cult of the robe" accounted for nearly one-third of the conversation. Yet, when covering her confirmation, journalists made mention of topics related to this category only 12.8% of the time. Indeed, their attention to the "cult of personality" nearly matched the interest of the senators in her judicial philosophy (28.5% versus 32.1%) (see Figures 2.12 and 2.13).

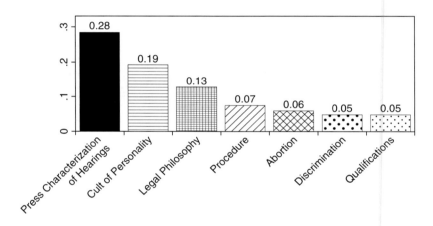

FIGURE 2.12 Distribution of Categories: Media Coverage of Sotomayor Hearings

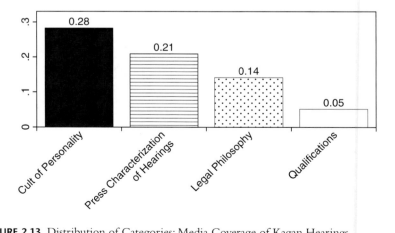

FIGURE 2.13 Distribution of Categories: Media Coverage of Kagan Hearings

Conclusion

When providing context and information regarding the hearings, the media's reporting is somewhat skewed, emphasizing a nominee's personality and certain issues, especially abortion. However, the themes present in this coverage are not made up out of whole cloth. The hearings do include references to the "cult of personality" as well as provocative and controversial issues like abortion and discrimination. Thus, the image of the confirmation and the eventual justice is distorted in the media's reports, but it is not distorted on the level of a funhouse mirror. The consumer of the news certainly will learn about much of the actual content of the confirmation hearings, and this stands to reason. The format and the openness of the hearings, as well as the public displays of the nominees all make for good and accessible copy. Transcripts are readily available. Senators often make themselves available to the media for interviews via press conferences. And this plays into the media's penchant for emphasizing the individual and unique personalities over other topics, including judicial philosophy and qualifications for the Bench. In a sense, then, the "justices as personalities" is a residue of the confirmation process. But what of the media's stories about the actual business of the Court where the justices toil behind the purple curtain and dole out orders and opinions on a timetable that is not designed to aid the media? Under these conditions, does the media provide more or less valid information about the Court's agenda and outputs? Does the "cult of personality" begin to fade? Or do the funhouse optics come even more to the fore? We take these questions up in the next chapter.

Notes

1 We, of course, argue that this trend is changing. Davis (2014) also notes that some of these norms may slowly be deteriorating, but there are still many Court reporters who remain faithful to this norm.

2 The "public" nature of confirmations to the Court is itself a recent phenomenon. Confirmation hearings were almost never public prior to the 1950s. All Senate debates over nominations were held in closed session unless two-thirds of the Senate voted otherwise until a rules change occurred in 1929. And television did not enter the process until Sandra Day O'Connor's nomination in 1981 (see Comiskey 2004; Davis 2011).

3 To be sure, these have become more or less common phenomena since Robert Bork's nomination in 1987, but they are not without historical antecedents. Davis (2011) points to the nominations of Louis Brandeis (1916) and John Parker (1930) as controversial and involving interest group campaigns in opposition.

4 Some presidents place more emphasis on ideological congruence than others (Diascro and Solberg 2009).

5 William Rehnquist received 26 and 33 negative votes for his initial appointment to the Court and then elevation to chief justice, respectively. David Souter received nine negative votes; Clarence Thomas, 48; Ruth Bader Ginsburg, three; Stephen Breyer, nine; Roberts, 22; Samuel Alito, 42; Sonia Sotomayor, 31; and Elena Kagan, 37.

34 Confirmation and the "Cult of Personality"

6 Here, and in all other instances of data collection and coding other than chapter 5, a team composed of one of the coauthors and trained research assistants conducted the coding. No individual coding was complete until a 95% rate of agreement was achieved between the coders. A coauthor individually coded the data in chapter 5.

7 Watson and Stookey (1988) originally created five roles: the Evaluator, Partisan, Validator (validating the senator's views regarding the nominee), Educator, and Advertiser. In their later work (1995), the final two roles were collapsed into the Advocate.

8 The four most recent Supreme Court nomination hearings follow recent experience where the president's party also held a majority in the Senate.

9 The Senate is polarizing more slowly than the House, but the increasing distance between the parties is still affecting behavior in the upper chamber. One need only consider the tortuous route the Obama administration and the Senate Democrats had to follow in order to enact health care legislation to appreciate the growing polarization in the Senate (Rockman, Waltenburg, and Campbell 2011).

10 Unless otherwise noted, all quotations from senators are drawn from the official transcripts of the confirmation hearings.

11 The ABA report on Alito noted the error and that the incident was not indicative of the judge. Screening processes, Alito explained to the committee, failed. Hatch quotes this report at length in the hearings.

12 Of course, it is impossible to disentangle a "gender" effect from partisan dynamics in the case of these hearings.

13 This category includes any discussion of constitutional issues of discrimination (e.g., the Fourteenth Amendment, or affirmative action) and statutes passed to prohibit discrimination (e.g., *Equal Pay Act*, the ADA).

14 After sarcastic questioning by Senator Charles Schumer in the third day of the hearings, we learned that John Roberts's favorite movies are *Doctor Zhivago* and *North by Northwest*.

15 To be sure, the Committee vote belies this neutrality. The vote broke down along party lines, with only Lindsey Graham crossing party lines to vote in favor of all four nominees. Three Democrats crossed lines to vote for Roberts (Senators Leahy, Kohl, and Feingold), but they all opposed Alito.

16 Robert Barnes and Paul Kane, "Sen. Graham's Exchanges With Sotomayor Among Most Anticipated of Judiciary Panel," *Washington Post*, July 17, 2009, www.washington post.com/wp-dyn/content/article/2009/07/16/AR2009071604123.html (last accessed March 21, 2014).

17 In 2008 Senator Amy Klobuchar from Minnesota joined her. Following the typical pattern of freshman senators, Senator Klobuchar spoke less frequently and was barely mentioned in the press.

18 Senator Schumer does not fit as neatly into this typology. However, he is something of a celebrity by Washington standards, and is a ready source for the media. Indeed, Bob Dole once quipped that the most dangerous place in Washington is between Charles Schumer and a camera.

19 Indeed, even if we add together all the attributions and quotes, their sum exceeds the reporter-led sentences by only 109.

20 Ann Gerhart, "Sotomayor Warms the Hearing Room With a Confident Touch," *Washington Post*, July 15, 2009: A10 (accessed via Lexis on November 30, 2011).

21 NBC Transcripts from the *Today Show*, "Confirmation Hearings Continue Today for Elena Kagan," June 29, 2010; Robert Barnes and Amy Goldstein, "Republicans Grill Nominee but Say They Expect Approval," *Washington Post*, July 1, 2010: A4.

22 Since Ronald Reagan, the GOP has placed in their party platform a commitment to selecting judges who interpret the Constitution strictly.

23 Robert Barnes and Amy Goldstein, "Republicans Grill Nominee but Say They Expect Approval," *Washington Post*, July 1, 2010: A4.

References

Bond, Jon R., and Richard Fleisher. 2000. *Polarized Politics: Congress and the President in a Partisan Era*. Washington, DC: CQ Press.

Comiskey, Michael. 2004. *Seeking Justice: The Judging of Supreme Court Nominees*. Lawrence: University Press of Kansas.

Davis, Richard. 2011. *Justices and Journalists: The U.S. Supreme Court and the Media*. New York: Cambridge University Press.

———. ed. 2014. *Covering the United States Supreme Court in the Digital Age*. New York: Cambridge University Press.

Diascro, Jennifer Segal, and Rorie Spill Solberg. 2009. "George W. Bush's Legacy on the Federal Bench: Policy in the Face of Diversity." *Judicature* 92:289–301.

Epstein, Lee, William M. Landes, and Richard A. Posner. 2010. "Inferring the Winning Party in the Supreme Court from the Pattern of Questioning in Oral Argument." *Journal of Legal Studies* 39 (2):433–67.

Epstein, Lee, Rene Lindstadt, Jeffrey A. Segal, and Chad Westerland. 2006. "The Changing Dynamics of Senate Voting on Supreme Court Nominees." *Journal of Politics* 68 (2):296–307.

Epstein, Lee, and Jeffrey A. Segal. 2007. *Advice and Consent: The Politics of Judicial Appointments*. New York: Oxford University Press.

Glickstein, Jed. 2012. "After Midnight: The Circuit Judges and the Repeal of the Judiciary Act of 1801." *Yale Journal of Law and Humanities* 24 (2):543–78.

Mayhew, David R. 1974. *Congress: The Electoral Connection*. New Haven, CT: Yale University Press.

McCarty, Nolan, Keith T. Poole, and Howard Rosenthal. 2006. *Polarized America: The Dance of Ideology and Unequal Riches*. Cambridge, MA: MIT Press.

McCormick, James M., and Eugene R. Wittkopf. 1990. "Bipartisanship, Partisanship, and Ideology in Congressional-Executive Foreign Policy Relations, 1947–1988." *Journal of Politics* 52 (4):1077–1100.

O'Brien, David M. 2005. *Storm Center: The Supreme Court in American Politics*. New York: W.W. Norton.

Poole, Keith T., and Howard Rosenthal. 1991. "Patterns of Congressional Voting." *American Journal of Political Science* 35 (1):228–78.

Rockman, Bert A., Eric N. Waltenburg, and Colin Campbell. 2011. "Presidential Style and the Obama Presidency." In *The Obama Presidency: Appraisals and Prospects*, pp. 331–352. eds. B. A. Rockman, A. Rudolevige, and C. Campbell. Washington, DC: CQ Press.

Segal, Jeffrey A., Charles M. Cameron, and Albert D. Cover. 1992. "A Spatial Model of Roll Call Voting: Senators, Constituents, Presidents, and Interest Groups in Supreme Court Confirmations." *American Journal of Political Science* 36 (1):96–121.

Segal, Jeffrey A., and Harold J. Spaeth. 2002. *The Supreme Court and the Attitudinal Model Revisited*. New York: Cambridge University Press.

Segal, Jeffrey A., Harold J. Spaeth, and Sara C. Benesh. 2005. *The Supreme Court in the American Legal System*. New York: Cambridge University Press.

Sinclair, Barbara. 2006. *Party Wars: Polarization and the Politics of National Policy Making*. Norman: University of Oklahoma Press.

Smith, Steven S., and Christopher J. Deering. 1997. *Committees in Congress*. 3rd ed. Washington, DC: CQ Press.

Soroka, Stuart N. 2012. "The Gatekeeping Function: Distributions of Information in Media and the Real World." *Journal of Politics* 74 (2):514–28.

Watson, George L., and John A. Stookey. 1988. "Supreme Court Confirmation Hearings: A View from the Senate." *Judicature* 71 (4):186–96.

———. 1995. *Shaping America: The Politics of Supreme Court Appointments*. New York: HarperCollins College.

Weisberg, Herbert F. 1978. "Evaluating Theories of Congressional Roll-Call Voting." *American Journal of Political Science* 22 (3):554–77.

3

THE DECISIONAL MYTH

As we noted in chapter 2, the Supreme Court's decision making is conducted out of the public's sight and, in most instances, out of its mind. The justices, however, do announce their docketing and merits decisions at various points over the Court's term. Indeed, oral argument and opinion announcements are the only two relatively open forums available to observe Supreme Court business, although one needs either tickets or a press pass to watch even these. Ultimately, these forums are but small glimpses into the world behind the purple curtain; the press, however, takes what it is given and uses these opportunities to relay happenings at the Court. "Today at the Supreme Court" is a favored refrain of broadcast media anchors[1] and is used to introduce stories that elucidate the mysterious work of the justices—stories covering grants of certiorari, decisions on the merits, and oral arguments.

How often does the work of the Court deserve, in the eyes of the media, the public's attention? And do the decisions that are covered provide an accurate accounting of the Court's work? We explore these questions in this chapter following a fairly direct path. After a brief discussion of our data, their sources, and collection methodology, we turn to a broad description of the landscape of the Court's merits outputs. Having charted the actual topography of the Court's work, we then move to an analysis of the media's portrayal of it. We find that the media present a somewhat distorted image of the Court's work. To be sure, the media outlets we examine report on the lion's share of the Court's merits decisions. (Indeed, nearly three-quarters of the Court's merits decisions announced during the terms we analyze are mentioned in at least one story.) However, the media appreciably overreport some decisions depending upon the nature of the issue raised in the case. We also find that there is a greater likelihood of the media

38 The Decisional Myth

reporting on the political and personal surrounding a case. We conclude by offering some suggestions as to whether the nature of the press's coverage of the Court and its work affects the public's attitudes about the Third Branch.

The Data

In recent years, pollsters and scholars have noted a steady decline in the public's support for the Court and its work. Supreme Court approval still significantly outpaces the public's approval of Congress, but now hovers in territory that would be considered problematic for an occupant of the White House. In July 2013, Gallup reported that the Court's approval is near an all-time low (46%), with only 31% of Republicans supporting this conservative Court.[2] To be sure, there are a multitude of explanations for the decided drop in the mass public's support for the Court (in 2001, approval was 59%); however, as the media is the conduit by which most people find out about the work of the Court, the nature of the media's coverage of it likely contributes to this alarming trend (on the media and the Court see Baird and Gangl 2006; Clawson and Waltenburg 2009; Franklin and Kosaki 1995; Gibson and Caldeira 2011; Gibson, Lodge, and Woodson 2012; Johnston and Bartels 2010; on media effects more generally, see Bartels 1993). Examining coverage of the Court may not explain the public's declining love for it, but if we discern significant changes in the coverage of the Court over time, we may be taking a first step toward identifying one important explanatory factor.

It is our supposition that the media's choices about what to cover and how to cover it provide a skewed picture of the work of the Court and undermines the Court's position on its apolitical pedestal. To discern the gap, or lack thereof, between the media's presentation of the work of the Court and its actual docket, as well as any increased association with politics or partisanship in this display, we examine newsprint and broadcast stories using a pseudo rolling cross-section approach.[3]

Specifically, we collected data from stories covering Supreme Court decisions over six separate Court terms spanning three chief justices and from four major news sources (the *New York Times*, the *Washington Post*, the *Los Angeles Times*, and the *CBS Evening News*). The three papers are national papers, with the *New York Times* and the *Washington Post* perceived as leaning left and the *Los Angeles Times* leaning right (see Segal et al. 1995). We use the *CBS Evening News* for two reasons. First, although today we could include several of the 24-hour news channels and various Internet-based sites, these media did not exist over most of our time period. Second, CBS transcripts were more complete and more available than those of other two major broadcast networks.[4] In terms of paring down the study, we only collected data on news stories that contained information about a Supreme Court decision, merits or otherwise. While including stories covering oral argument or certiorari decisions would have produced a more complete accounting of the media's coverage of the Court's business, we selected stories on merits decisions and orders as our unit of analysis because oral argument and certiorari decisions do not produce "law." Indeed, even with this winnowing we collected data on nearly 2,000 stories, covering over 500 Court decisions.

What's on the Docket?

Perhaps the best place to begin our analysis is to establish the basic terrain of the Court's work by describing its outputs—both in terms of the number of cases decided and the nature of the cases decided—for the terms under review. As most students of the Court know, the productivity of the Court is in decline. In the current century, the justices are accepting fewer cases for review and rendering fewer decisions than in earlier Court terms. This point is clearly illustrated in Figure 3.1.

What of the issue composition of the Court's decisional agenda? Using the value categories from the *U.S. Supreme Court Database* to identify broad issue areas, we see some change in the composition of the docket. In 1975, cases concerning judicial power and criminal procedure top the Court's agenda. Economic and civil rights cases followed fairly closely with due process and First Amendment cases making somewhat frequent appearances. For the other twentieth-century terms, the distribution of categories across the docket is not stable, but neither is it marked by striking changes. The civil rights category may be the only exception to this observation; the incidence of cases involving it bounces around substantially across the six terms reported (see Table 3.1). Finally, we note that entering the twenty-first century there is a decided jump in economic cases with a similar drop in First Amendment cases. Otherwise, the docket remains remarkably consistent.[5]

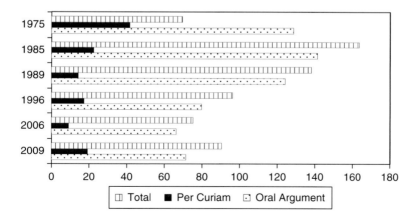

FIGURE 3.1 Distribution of Supreme Court Output, Various Terms

40 The Decisional Myth

TABLE 3.1 Distribution of Court Output by Issue Area

	1975	1985	1989	1996	2006	2009
Issue						
Criminal Procedure	37	46	39	19	21	33
Economic Activity	32	16	23	16	21	20
Civil Rights	30	31	9	20	6	10
Judicial Power	39	23	19	12	16	11
First Amendment	13	14	14	5	3	5
Due Process	14	7	4	5	0	1
Federalism	6	10	9	7	1	3
Unions	5	4	5	1	2	3
Federal Taxation	1	5	7	3	2	0
Privacy	3	2	4	7	1	1
Attorneys	0	4	4	0	2	4
Misc.	0	1	0	0	0	0

What's in the News?

Given the decline in the Court's discretionary work, we could imagine two opposite effects in terms of media coverage. First, the media could cover the same amount of cases overall—a smaller docket simply translating into coverage of a greater portion of that docket without an increase in column inches or broadcast minutes over time. Alternatively, the decrease in Court output may signal a concomitant decrease in attention or perceived importance by the media leading to less coverage overall. The data reported in Table 3.2 suggest the latter pattern holds. They are also consistent with the observations of Lyle Denniston, the veteran Court reporter:

> We are in the early stages of a, perhaps, really profound shift in which the press attention to the Court, the press awareness of the Court . . . is going to be so much smaller over time . . . in the last ten years, the American newspaper scope of coverage of the Supreme Court of the United States has declined markedly. (Denniston qtd. in Strickler 2014, 155)

In 1975, all of the media included in our study reported on a total of 140 unique cases (83% of the total of orally argued or per curiam decisions). In 1985, the number drops to 118 (72%); and in 1989 it drops again to 103, although a slightly greater percentage of the docket is covered (75%). In 1996, the decline in the absolute number of cases continues, with the media covering only 59 cases—61% of the Court's output. The percentage rises a bit for 2006 to 64%; but with only 48 cases covered, this increase is due to the smaller docket, not a marked increase in the absolute number of stories about Court decisions. By the

The Decisional Myth **41**

TABLE 3.2 Total Unique Cases Covered by Medium

Medium	1975	1985	1989	1996	2006	2009
CBS	32	25	21	14	8	6
New York Times	120	71	90	52	39	34
Washington Post & **Los Angeles Times**	158	165	108	60	55	47
All Media	310	261	219	126	102	87

October Term 2009, our four outlets covered only 43 cases—less than one-half of the total docket (48%). In summation, the pattern in absolute numbers is one of declining attention to a decreased docket of the Court among our archetypical media sources.

We can break down this coverage even further by examining CBS, our representative broadcast medium, the *New York Times*, and the *Washington Post* and *Los Angeles Times* combined. Upon examining these frequencies two things are clear. First, as found previously (Spill and Oxley 2003), the *New York Times* earns its title as "the paper of record," at least as far as coverage of the Supreme Court is concerned. The *New York Times* consistently covers a greater number of cases in its pages and generally publishes more stories on these cases (see Table 3.2 and Tables 3.3a through 3.3f). Indeed, the *New York Times* covers almost 56% of the total number of decisions across our six terms of analysis. Additionally, the *New York Times* provides more content about the majority opinion, a case's facts and history, and the margin of the vote than do its counterparts.[6] Second, we find a similar temporal pattern regarding the incidence of cases covered among the individual media outlets. To state it simply, the number of overall cases each media source reports on goes down. It appears that a smaller docket does not translate into a larger portion of the Court's work making news.

The story thus far is one of lessening coverage. These total numbers, however, do not reveal the frequency of individual stories about cases deemed newsworthy. For example, in 1975 our four representative media[7] ran 548 stories that had at least one sentence describing a decision of the Court, and even in the later, leaner years the number still tops 170. Whether this is due to the Court's smaller agenda or the market competition from cable news and Internet sources, we cannot know. Interestingly, what is lost in the downsizing of Court reporting are the shorter stories; the mean number of sentences per story/year increases from 28 (1975) to 32 (2009) and is highest in October Term 2006 at 42.

TABLE 3.3A Total Stories and Unique Docket Numbers for October Term 1975

Criminal	57	33	8	31	129
Procedure	(29/37)	(24/37)	(7/37)	(18/37)	(32/37)
Civil Rights	56	26	14	19	115
	(26/30)	(21/30)	(9/30)	(13/30)	(30/30)
First	45	56	15	15	131
Amendment	(12/13)	(13/13)	(7/13)	(8/13)	(13/13)
Due Process	13	11	0	6	30
	(8/14)	(10/14)	(0/14)	(6/14)	(11/14)
Privacy	6	5	1	2	14
	(3/3)	(2/3)	(1/3)	(1/3)	(3/3)
Attorneys	0	0	0	0	0
	(0/0)	(0/0)	(0/0)	(0/0)	(0/0)
Unions	9	4	1	4	18
	(4/5)	(3/5)	(1/5)	(1/5)	(4/5)
Economic	32	13	4	13	62
Activity	(20/32)	(13/32)	(4/32)	(11/32)	(24/32)
Judicial Power	22	6	4	10	42
	(15/39)	(6/39)	(2/39)	(6/39)	(20/39)
Federalism	3	2	1	0	6
	(2/6)	(2/6)	(1/6)	(0/6)	(2/6)
Federal	1	0	0	0	1
Taxation	(1/1)	(0/1)	(0/1)	(0/1)	(1/1)
Miscellaneous	0	0	0	0	0
	(0/0)	(0/0)	(0/0)	(0/0)	(0/0)

[1] The top number in each cell represents the total number of stories. The numerator in the ratio is the number of unique dockets covered by that medium and the denominator is the number of decided cases.

TABLE 3.3B Total Stories and Unique Docket Numbers for October Term 1985

Criminal	20	28	2	27	77
Procedure	(18/46)	(26/46)	(2/46)	(21/46)	(33/46)
Civil Rights	24	43	9	27	103
	(15/31)	(17/31)	(9/31)	(13/31)	(21/31)
First	7	12	3	20	42
Amendment	(7/14)	(11/14)	(3/14)	(5/14)	(14/14)
Due Process	3	4	1	7	15
	(3/7)	(4/7)	(1/7)	(5/7)	(6/7)
Privacy	8	9	2	4	23
	(2/2)	(2/2)	(2/2)	(2/2)	(2/2)
Attorneys	3	2	1	3	9
	(3/4)	(2/4)	(1/4)	(2/4)	(4/4)
Unions	2	2	0	1	5
	(2/4)	(2/4)	(0/4)	(1/4)	(3/4)

Economic Activity	8 (7/16)	8 (8/16)	2 (2/16)	8 (5/16)	26 (10/16)
Judicial Power	5 (5/23)	9 (8/23)	3 (3/23)	5 (4/23)	22 (10/23)
Federalism	4 (4/10)	7 (7/10)	1 (1/10)	9 (4/10)	21 (9/10)
Federal Taxation	5 (4/5)	3 (2/5)	0 (0/5)	4 (4/5)	12 (5/5)
Miscellaneous	3 (1/1)	7 (1/1)	1 (1/1)	3 (1/1)	14 (1/1)

[1] The top number in each cell represents the total number of stories. The numerator in the ratio is the number of unique dockets covered by that medium and the denominator is the number of decided cases.

TABLE 3.3C Total Stories and Unique Docket Numbers for October Term 1989

Criminal Procedure	49 (26/39)	15 (13/39)	9 (6/39)	46 (21/39)	119 (30/39)
Civil Rights	12 (5/9)	4 (3/9)	2 (2/9)	16 (7/9)	36 (7/9)
First Amendment	40 (14/14)	5 (3/14)	8 (7/14)	49 (9/14)	102 (14/14)
Due Process	4 (4/4)	2 (2/4)	0 (0/4)	5 (3/4)	11 (4/4)
Privacy	8 (4/4)	5 (2/4)	3 (2/4)	12 (4/4)	28 (4/4)
Attorneys	1 (1/4)	0 (0/4)	0 (0/4)	0 (0/4)	1 (1/4)
Unions	1 (1/5)	2 (2/5)	00/5	2 (1/5)	5 (2/5)
Economic Activity	20 (15/23)	6 (6/23)	2 (2/23)	18 (11/23)	46 (17/23)
Judicial Power	26 (8/19)	6 (6/19)	1 (1/19)	17 (7/19)	50 (11/19)
Federalism	9 (8/9)	1 (1/9)	1 (1/9)	8 (4/9)	19 (8/9)
Federal Taxation	7 (4/7)	1 (1/7)	0 (0/7)	4 (2/7)	12 (5/7)
Miscellaneous	0 (0/0)	0 (0/0)	0 (0/0)	0 (0/0)	0 (0/0)

[1] The top number in each cell represents the total number of stories. The numerator in the ratio is the number of unique dockets covered by that medium and the denominator is the number of decided cases.

TABLE 3.3D Total Stories and Unique Docket Numbers for October Term 1996

Criminal	18	8	1	3	30
Procedure	(10/19)	(6/19)	(1/19)	(3/19)	(11/19)
Civil Rights	15	13	3	2	33
	(10/20)	(8/20)	(3/20)	(2/20)	(12/20)
First	15	23	4	14	56
Amendment	(5/5)	(5/5)	(3/5)	(4/5)	(5/5)
Due Process	7	4	0	0	11
	(5/5)	(2/5)	(0/5)	(3/4)	(5/5)
Privacy	29	20	5	15	69
	(6/7)	(6/7)	(4/7)	(4/7)	(6/7)
Attorneys	0	0	0	0	0
	(0/0)	(0/0)	(0/0)	(0/0)	(0/0)
Unions	0	0	0	0	0
	(0/1)	(0/1)	(0/1)	(0/1)	(0/1)
Economic	22	19	1	12	54
Activity	(6/16)	(6/16)	(1/16)	(3/16)	(8/16)
Judicial Power	9	5	2	3	19
	(5/12)	(3/12)	(1/12)	(2/12)	(6/12)
Federalism	5	10	2	1	18
	(3/7)	(3/7)	(1/7)	(1/7)	(3/7)
Federal	1	2	0	1	4
Taxation	(1/3)	(2/3)	(0/3)	(1/3)	(2/3)
Miscellaneous	0	0	0	0	0
	(0/0)	(0/0)	(0/0)	(0/0)	(0/0)

[1] The top number in each cell represents the total number of stories. The numerator in the ratio is the number of unique dockets covered by that medium and the denominator is the number of decided cases.

TABLE 3.3E Total Stories and Unique Docket Numbers for October Term 2006

Criminal	19	6	1	9	35
Procedure	(13/21)	(4/21)	(1/21)	(7/21)	(13/21)
Civil Rights	14	6	1	12	33
	(4/6)	(3/6)	(1/6)	(5/6)	(5/6)
First	8	5	2	6	21
Amendment	(3/3)	(3/3)	(2/3)	(3/3)	(3/3)
Due Process	0	0	0	0	0
	(0/0)	(0/0)	(0/0)	(0/0)	(0/0)
Privacy	16	5	3	10	34
	(1/1)	(1/1)	(1/1)	(1/1)	(1/1)
Attorneys	0	0	0	0	0
	(0/2)	(0/2)	(0/2)	(0/2)	(0/2)
Unions	1	0	0	2	3
	(1/2)	(0/2)	(0/2)	(2/2)	(2/2)

Economic Activity	18 (10/21)	16 (11/21)	1 (1/21)	11 (8/21)	46 (17/21)
Judicial Power	18 (6/16)	7 (3/16)	2 (2/16)	8 (3/16)	35 (6/16)
Federalism	1 (1/1)	2 (1/1)	0 (0/1)	0 (0/1)	3 (1/1)
Federal Taxation	0 (0/2)	0 (0/2)	0 (0/2)	0 (0/2)	0 (0/2)
Miscellaneous	0 (0/0)	0 (0/0)	0 (0/0)	0 (0/0)	0 (0/0)

[1] The top number in each cell represents the total number of stories. The numerator in the ratio is the number of unique dockets covered by that medium and the denominator is the number of decided cases.

TABLE 3.3F Total Stories and Unique Docket Numbers for October Term 2009

Criminal Procedure	23 (14/33)	13 (11/33)	5 (3/33)	8 (5/33)	49 (17/33)
Civil Rights	3 (3/10)	4 (4/10)	0 (0/10)	1 (1/10)	8 (4/10)
First Amendment	24 (5/5)	12 (5/5)	4 (2/5)	11 (4/5)	51 (5/5)
Due Process	1 (1/1)	1 (1/1)	0 (0/1)	2 (1/1)	4 (1/1)
Privacy	1 (1/1)	1 (1/1)	0 (0/1)	1 (1/1)	3 (1/1)
Attorneys	2 (2/4)	2 (2/4)	0 (0/4)	0 (0/4)	4 (2/4)
Unions	0 (0/3)	1 (1/3)	0 (0/3)	0 (0/3)	1 (1/3)
Economic Activity	6 (5/20)	4 (4/20)	0 (0/20)	2 (1/20)	12 (8/20)
Judicial Power	1 (1/11)	2 (2/11)	0 (0/11)	1 (1/11)	4 (2/11)
Federalism	3 (2/3)	2 (1/3)	1 (1/3)	1 (1/3)	7 (2/3)
Federal Taxation	0 (0/0)	0 (0/0)	0 (0/0)	0 (0/0)	0 (0/0)
Miscellaneous	0 (0/0)	0 (0/0)	0 (0/0)	0 (0/0)	0 (0/0)

[1] The top number in each cell represents the total number of stories. The numerator in the ratio is the number of unique dockets covered by that medium and the denominator is the number of decided cases.

46 The Decisional Myth

For our investigation, however, neither the total number of cases covered nor the total number of news stories presented is particularly germane. Our supposition is that whatever coverage there is of the Court's work, that coverage is skewed in a way that may undermine, or at least balance, the "cult of the robe" by presenting the Court as "just another political institution" staffed by politicians and steeped in current political controversies (Gibson and Cladeira 2009; Scheb and Lyons 2001). To test this hypothesis, we now turn our attention to the substance of the media coverage. Here, we again employ the value categories used in the *U.S. Supreme Court Database* to compare the complexion of the docket with the media's portrayal of it. In essence, we explore whether the media presents a caricature of the Court's work or a still life.

Certainly since the "switch in time" post-New Deal, the justices have devoted a significant portion of their docket to civil rights and liberties questions. In terms of the database categories, this broad issue area encompasses criminal procedure, civil rights, First Amendment, due process, and privacy. And as Table 3.1 indicates, this conventional wisdom regarding the Court's business is borne out. Figure 3.2 displays a word cloud; it aggregates the data for our six terms and provides a visual indicator of the issue areas more prominently on the docket. Issue areas appearing in a larger font occurred more frequently. Now, we would expect the media to overreport these decisions in these issue areas, inasmuch as they are "racier" cases, oftentimes packed with emotionally charged, socially significant issues and controversies. (For the tendency of the media to devote greater coverage to cases that are more socially significant, see Vining and Marcin 2014, 184.) Our concern is with the extent to which this overreporting occurs, once we disaggregate from the global civil rights and liberties nomenclature.

We identified the total number of stories and the total number of unique docket numbers each medium covered for all six terms and report these data in Tables 3.3a through 3.3f. In the tables, the total number of unique docket numbers for each area is displayed in the parentheses over the total number of unique cases heard by the Court in that same term. The total number of stories is reported in each cell above this ratio. A quick perusal of these tables reveals that there are indeed some elements of caricature in the news. This exaggerated picture of the Court's work comes in two forms. First, there is the dissonance between the actual docket and the stories receiving coverage. The ratio of decisions covered to cases

FIGURE 3.2 Aggregate Word Cloud Issue Distribution of Docket

FIGURE 3.3 Aggregate Word Cloud Issue Distribution of News Stories

decided is variable in each issue area over the years studied, and this comes as no great surprise. After all, each term is unique and the big issue area in one term does not necessarily presage what will garner attention during the next. However, there does seem to be a tendency to cover a greater proportion of the civil rights and liberties cases than other issue areas. In terms where this is less true, the exaggerated coverage simply switches to an alternative issue area, while one or two of the categories within the civil rights and liberties domain always remain saturated. Inspecting Figure 3.2 versus Figure 3.3 (another word cloud) yields an aggregate comparison of the composition of the docket with the composition of the news coverage in terms of issue area. Most notable is the substantial difference in the size of the fonts for the First Amendment, civil rights, and privacy categories between the two figures. In the word cloud depicting the media's coverage, the fonts for these categories are noticeably larger.

With respect to the broadcast media, as CBS's coverage of the Court dwindles over time, this gap between decisions and stories attenuates. The number of stories more closely matches the number of cases covered; however, the number of cases covered is, in our opinion, dismal. This same trend over time also is present in the newsprint media, but the decline in overall cases and coverage is not as extreme.

Second, the newsprint media are more likely to beat the proverbial dead horse in some issue areas. Take, for example, the October Term 1975. Here, the *New York Times* and *Washington Post* covered almost all or all of the First Amendment cases respectively. In the *Times* 12 decisions were covered in 45 separate stories (nearly four stories per decision); and 13 cases, the entirety of the docket in this issue area, were covered in 56 individual stories in the *Post* (over four stories per decision).[8] Similarly, in the October Term 2009, the Court decided only five First Amendment cases. However, 25 separate stories mentioning a First Amendment decision appeared in the *New York Times*; 12 stories appeared in the *Post*. (Both of these outlets covered all five cases.) The *Los Angeles Times* covered four of the cases and published 11 separate articles on these decisions. Bringing up the rear, CBS covered only two of the cases, but four stories were broadcast.

Examining this oversaturation more closely, there is no doubt that these issue areas justify multiple stories. We next investigate whether individual cases

48 The Decisional Myth

reasonably serve as "news pegs" (see Clawson, Strine, and Waltenburg 2003). To discern whether a case is indeed a news peg, we calculated the mean number of stories and the standard deviation for each newspaper medium for each of our six terms. To determine the threshold for a news peg, we added one and a half standard deviations to the mean. If a case generated that many stories or more, it ranks as a news peg. Our measure, though simple, takes into consideration the differences in coverage and docket across our mediums and the Court's terms. We excluded CBS from the analyses because the network generally covered so few cases that, with the possible exception of *Buckley v. Valeo* (424 U.S. 1 [1976]), no case surmounted the threshold. In total we found 62 news pegs across the three newspapers—16 from the *New York Times*, 21 from the *Washington Post*, and 25 from the *Los Angeles Times* (see Table 3.4).

Recall from Table 3.1 that the Court heard 128 cases with oral argument in the October Term 1975. Of these cases, only nine were the source of unique news pegs (<1%). All three papers substantially overreported on *Buckley v. Valeo*. *Buckley* voided campaign finance regulations and public financing in the middle of a presidential primary season. The implications of the decision on the election and the subsequent congressional actions were obviously newsworthy and harkened back to the Court's decision. The *New York Times* and the *Los Angeles Times* had news pegs from *Gregg v. Georgia* (428 U.S. 153 [1976]). Interestingly, not only did the *Los Angeles Times* create more news pegs, it did so in several unique cases in less salient issue areas. For example, only the *Los Angeles Times*

TABLE 3.4 News Pegs by Term and Newspaper

	New York Times	*Washington Post*	*Los Angeles Times*
1975	6 [3]	8[1]	3 [8]
	2, 2.3	1.7, 3.6	1.6, 1
1985	3 [5]	4 [7]	3 [6]
	1.3, .8	1.5, 1.3	1.6, .7
1989	5 [3]	3 [3]	6 [6]
	2, 1.8	1.2, .7	2.6, 2
1996	3 [2]	7 [5]	5 [1]
	1.3, .6	2.7, 2.8	2.3, 1.4
2006	7 [2]	4 [3]	5 [3]
	2.4, 2.8	1.8, 1.2	2, 1.9
2009	7 [1]	3 [2]	4 [1]
	1.9, 2.9	1.3, 1.1	1.8, 1.9
Total News Pegs	16	21	25

[1] For each year, the first number in a cell is the news peg threshold, rounded up to the nearest whole number. The number in brackets is the number of cases that meet that threshold. The second set of numbers is the mean and the standard deviation. For example, in 1989, the news peg threshold for the *New York Times* is 5 stories. Three cases meet that threshold; the mean is 2 and the standard deviation is 1.8.

made a news peg out of *Michelin Tire Corp. v. Wages* (423 U.S. 276 [1976]), where the Court determined that Georgia could indeed lay a nondiscriminatory ad valorem property tax on imported goods held by Michelin in that state; and *National League of Cities v. Usery* (426 U.S. 833 [1976]), where the Court curtailed the ability of the federal government to regulate states directly. Whereas the *New York Times*, in its one unique news peg, spent column inches on *Carla A. Hills, Secretary of Housing and Urban Development v. Gautreaux* (425 U.S. 284 [1976]). This potentially explosive decision determined that the Department of Housing and Urban Development discriminated in its placement of low-income housing and that a remedy for segregated housing, which was limited to a single metropolitan area, was impermissible. The purported ripple effects for property values, construction contracts, and other potential areas of discrimination merited significant coverage.

In the October Term 1985, all five cases that were news pegs in the *New York Times* were also news pegs in the *Washington Post*, with three of the cases appearing multiple times in all three papers' pages. The *Post* had two unique news pegs; both cases dealt with claims of discrimination. The *Los Angeles Times* had three unique news pegs. During this term, the Court heard 141 cases with oral argument. While the newspapers may provide oversaturated coverage in specific issue areas, it does not appear that they home in on only one or two cases. News pegs emerged from less than 1% of all the cases during this term.

In the October Term 1989, our media outlets produced 11 unique news pegs, with the *Los Angeles Times* once again focusing on more cases than the other two papers. In this term, the Court heard 124 cases with argument, so the 11 news pegs covered less than 1% of the Court's total output. The only case that achieved news peg status across the media outlets during this term, not surprisingly, was *U.S. v. Eichman* (496 U.S. 310 [1990]). In *Eichman* the Court voided the federal *Flag Protection Act of 1989*, ruling that flag desecration is a form of free expression that is covered by the Constitution.

As the docket decreased, so did the news pegs. In October Terms 1996 and 2006, the Court heard 79 and 66 cases with argument respectively. Only 10 cases generated news pegs over these two terms, and no case from the 1996 term was covered in this fashion by all three newspapers. The *New York Times* and the *Washington Post* pegged *Clinton v. Jones* (520 U.S. 681 [1997]), whereas the *Post* and the *Los Angeles Times* pegged *Washington v. Glucksberg* (521 U.S. 702 [1997])—the first physician-assisted suicide case to reach the High Court. In 2006, the *New York Times* pegged only two cases, and both the *Post* and the *Los Angeles Times* joined it in this action—pegging *Massachusetts v. Environmental Protection Agency* (549 U.S. 497 [2007]) and *Gonzales v. Carhart* (550 U.S. 124 [2007]). *Massachusetts* found the EPA on the losing side when the Court ruled that the agency does have the authority to regulate greenhouse gas emissions under the *Clean Air Act*; in *Carhart*, the Court upheld the federal ban on partial birth abortions.

50 The Decisional Myth

By the October Term 2009, news pegs based upon Court cases are significantly thin on the ground. Only two cases generate pegs with one covered by all three papers (*Citizens United v. Federal Election Commission*, 558 U.S. 310 [2010]). The ruling itself was important as it altered decades of precedent by holding that corporations can spend unlimited amounts of money in independent expenditures during political campaigns under the First Amendment. The case, however, perhaps was destined to become a news peg after President Obama mentioned the case during his 2011 State of the Union address. The public chastising of the Court by the president would itself gather coverage, but this peg was aided by Justice Alito's unfortunate habit of speaking to himself. He was caught on camera responding to the president's comments, and that uncharacteristic judicial behavior also generated press coverage.[9] In each of these stories, there was at least a sentence or two that referenced the case and its decisions—again, not a surprise that this case became a peg.

Now, by no means are we contending that the media should have covered these decisions *less* vigorously. We do suggest that there are real consequences for the Court based upon the media's use of these cases as news pegs. First, there is a significant correlation between the frequency of a given case's coverage and the average amount of attention per story the media gives both to the political justifications for the decision ($r = .12; p < .03$) and the political implication of the decision ($r = .42; p < .00$). Thus, more-frequently covered cases are associated with more-frequent references to elements of the "cult of personality." Second, media studies and analyses from political psychology have shown that more-frequent coverage of an issue, or for our purposes a case, places that issue higher on the public's agenda (McCombs 2005; Shanto, Peters, and Kinder 1982). More stories on First Amendment or privacy cases, for example, suggest that these cases are more important than others on the Court's docket. Thus, the overrepresentation of certain cases in the media's coverage of the Court's outputs may result in the impression that the Court's policy making augur is limited to a relatively small set of cases touching upon a specific issue domain. Political or constitutional importance and public salience, however, may not coincide. For example, the Rehnquist Court's federalism jurisprudence went virtually unnoticed by the public; yet, these decisions curtailed congressional power significantly. (Recall that only the *Los Angeles Times* made a news peg of *National League of Cities*. The state of California was the appellant in the companion case, *California v. Usery* [74–879].)[10]

Moving from the overall coverage of cases, we now examine various elements of the news stories. Our data collection efforts included noting not only mentions of the content of the decisions, but also any legal or extralegal justifications reported. Likewise, we noted any personal information provided about the justices, background and facts of the case, the vote, implications (both political and legal) of the decision, and any politics surrounding the issue, so long as they were only tangentially related to the decision. With respect to reporting on the general information about the case—that is, the content of the majority decision, the vote, and the facts and history of the case—there has been little to no change in the average number of sentences devoted to both the content of the decision and the vote across the terms of the Court we analyze.[11] These two content areas seem to be the staple of media stories about decisions, regardless of who is writing or what case is under scrutiny. Reporting on the facts and history of the case, however, has become more frequent over time, increasing from an average of about three and three-quarter sentences per story in 1975 to over four and one-half sentences per story by 2009. It also bears noting that there is virtually no space, column or air, devoted to concurring or dissenting opinions unless, of course, the story is an infrequent excerpt from the justices' opinions (see Table 3.5).

To facilitate the analysis of the justifications reported we grouped them into three broad categories—*legal/institutional* (a category comprising legal approaches such as founders' or congressional intent, precedent, and statutory and constitutional interpretation); *living constitution* (made up of balancing, pragmatism, and contemporary norms); and *political justifications* (justifications based upon the justice's ideology or personal viewpoint). Our snapshots of media coverage yield two main points. First, most stories contain little to no information about the justifications the justices provide for their decisions. Second, and of greater consequence to our analysis here, we see a trend wherein "cult of personality justifications" join the "cult of the robe" in stories reporting on Court decisions with increasing frequency. To put it in concrete terms, in the earlier terms, 1975 and 1985, *political justifications* were hovering near zero per story. In fact, in 1985 they were practically absent (Mn = .008). By 2009, the average increases by more than 300% (.3 mentions per story; t = 3.16). Reported references to *living constitution justifications* also show a significant increase; in 1975 the average is .09, and by 2009 the average increases to .5 (t = 3.51). At the same time, *legal/institutional justifications* remain fairly stable, averaging between almost two mentions in our earlier terms and one mention per story later on (t = 1.07 and does not obtain significance). These trends are similar across all three of our print sources; no one newspaper "out-justifies" the other. CBS, on the other hand, reports far fewer justifications of

TABLE 3.5 Average Number of Sentences per Story, Content of the Decision

Content of Decision	1975	1985	1989	1996	2006	2009
Majority Opinion	4.97	4.69	4.11	6.11	3.89	4.67
Vote	2.08	2.14	1.93	1.93	2.19	2.27
Facts / History[1]	3.77	3.96	4.74	6.69	5.35	4.59

[1] Analysis of variance tests result in a significant F statistic only for differences across the terms in the average number of sentences per story reporting on the facts and history of a case if the October Term 1996 is excluded. If 1996 is included, the ANOVA results report significant F statistics for the average number of sentences reporting on both the majority opinion and the facts and history of the case.

52 The Decisional Myth

any kind, and this stands to reason. Broadcast media are not conducive to providing long quotes from the justices or excerpting large portions of their opinions.

Our findings are consistent with earlier findings by Spill and Oxley (2003) and Davis (1994). The Court reporters[12]—the elite of the press corps who specialize in coverage of the Court—are significantly more likely to include the legal justifications used by the justices. The difference in the mean of Court reporters versus other staff or wire service reporters is .67 (t = 6.88)—a massively significant difference. As Davis noted, these reporters tend to have more legal training, leading to a better understanding of the significance of legal language (1994, 66–69). Given this training, it comes as no great surprise that these reporters cover the content of the majority decision (t = 9.73), history and facts of the case (t = 5.51), and the vote margin (t = 6.75) significantly more often than their wire service and staff reporter counterparts. As Spill and Oxley (2003) found, this subset of the press writes longer stories, even if they do not write more stories as a group. And we find this tendency in our data too. The difference between Court reporters and others is an average of 10.8 more sentences per story (t = 12.76). In other words, these reporters are allowed more room to explicate the opinions.

This exploration of the elements of the news stories also supports our contention that the "cult of personality," with its emphasis on politics and personal information about the justices, is becoming more common, and it bears noting that Court reporters have a large hand in shaping this trend (but see LaRowe and Hoekstra 2014, 247–48). First, the difference in the average number of sentences reporting political justification that are written by Court reporters as opposed to their staff/wire counterparts is .08 (t = 4.55)—another seriously significant difference.[13] And this statistic is perhaps of greater consequence when one recognizes that these mostly legally trained journalists are members of what Davis has identified as the "elite" press corps, and thus tend to set the tone for coverage of the Court for the rest of the news media.

Second, as displayed in Figure 3.4, there is a clear and fairly steep upward trend in the inclusion of political and personal information about the justices over time, a trend consistent with Graber's observation that "Newspeople have learned to snare the average reader's interest by giving most stories a personal touch" (1984, 87). The mean number of sentences making mention of this sort of information more than triples between 1975 and 2009, with a decidedly large jump in the frequency of these mentions at the close of the twentieth century (see Figure 3.4). Indeed, the difference in the means between the twentieth and twenty-first centuries (4.07) is blindingly significant with a t-value of 6.34. The *Los Angeles Times* stands out among the other outlets as less likely to include personal or political information on the justices in its stories. The *New York Times*, *Washington Post*, and *CBS Evening News*, on the other hand, are about equally likely to humanize the justices and their decisions by sprinkling their coverage with references to a justice's ideology, age, disposition, health, and other similar topics. Court reporters

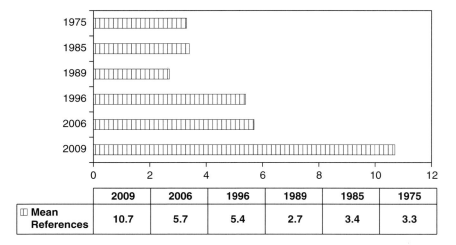

FIGURE 3.4 Mean References to Justices' Personal or Political Information per Story

are a bit more likely to employ these references (although the difference fails to attain conventional levels of significance), again supporting Davis's finding that, essentially, as Greenhouse (now Liptak) goes, so goes Court coverage.

Finally, when assessing the media's reporting on the implications of a Court decision, there are few patterns worthy of discussion. The media, when covering the Court, seems to be a "glass is half full" corps as they more often report who is helped than who is hurt by the policy (t = 2.57). In its broadcasts CBS devotes more attention to a decision's political implications than it does its legal ones, although the difference does not achieve statistical significance. There is no similar trend for the print media. Consistent with LaRowe and Hoekstra (2014), staff reporters are much more likely to cover a decision's political implications than any other member of the Court's press corps (t = 6.19). This finding is not terribly surprising given that a staff reporter is more likely steeped in politics and thus makes easy connections between case outcomes and political effects.

Conclusion

In conclusion, we do find significant differences across time, medium, and reporter in the coverage of the justices' final products. We also find the expected pattern of skewed presentations of the Court's overall agenda. More importantly, we find some strong evidence for the braiding of the two myths of the Court as our time series moves on. In the earliest term we examine, politics is divorced from Court coverage. Legal and political threads become closer and intertwined by the time John Roberts assumes the center chair. Is this trend responsible for the decline in support

54 The Decisional Myth

for the Court we referenced at the beginning of this chapter? Unfortunately, we do not have data that permit us to establish a causal chain of events. The circumstantial evidence presented here, however, suggests that this is at least causing some of this decline. As Gibson and Caldeira write, "the Supreme Court profits from a large store of . . . institutional support. To the extent that there is a threat to that support, it comes from events that challenge the view of the Court as a uniquely nonpolitical political institution" (2011, 200). We find that in its stories the media is increasingly including the politics of the Court as well as any politics surrounding the Court's decisions. Consequently, this trend in coverage may contribute to a demystification of the Court among the general public and a growing sense that the Court *is* a political institution. At the same time, though, the reporting continues to provide support for the "cult of the robe" in terms of the content of stories. Ultimately, it does not appear that the addition of politics is replacing the legal myth, and therefore the rise of the "cult of personality's" effect on the public's perception of the High Bench is mitigated. The stories do, however, present some cognitive dissonance to the audience by supporting both myths simultaneously. How the public processes these competing images is a question worthy of systematic analysis.

Notes

1 This observation is drawn from the data collected for this chapter and personal observation of broadcast coverage of the Court over the authors' adult lives.
2 See Andrew Dugan, "Americans' Approval of Supreme Court Near All-Time Low," Gallup, July 19, 2013, http://www.gallup.com/poll/163586/americans-approval-supreme-court-near-time-low.aspx (last accessed December 17, 2013). The same survey found the approval of the chief justice had fallen to its lowest recorded levels.
3 In terms of a rolling cross-section, we used a random number generator to select six terms over the tenures of Chief Justices Burger, Rehnquist, and Roberts. Thus we have a sample of news coverage over the course of six nonconsecutive terms.
4 We tried to collect data from NBC and ABC as well; however, their transcripts were not as complete in the databases available at Oregon State University, the University of Oregon, Arizona State University, and Purdue University. Indeed, even the CBS transcripts were unavailable for the 1975 and 1985 terms. For these, we searched the Vanderbilt News Archive abstracts and paid for compilation DVDs of the necessary stories. To do so for the other two major news broadcasts was cost prohibitive.
5 We recognize that using a rolling cross-section of terms may give an imprecise impression of docket stability or change.
6 We acknowledge that the *Washington Post* runs a close second, particularly in terms of vote margin and facts and history. In comparison to broadcast stories, the *Los Angeles Times* is also a champion of Court reporting.
7 By "representative," we by no means claim that these four media sources are *statistically* representative of the universe of media sources. We do contend that these three papers and one broadcast network capture the general trends of the national media over this time period.

8 Our unit of analysis here is the story/mention. If a news story mentions more than one decision, each decision was coded separately. Information that was general or applicable to both decisions would be included in both code sheets; data unique to each case would not be.

9 Justice Alito shook his head no and apparently mouthed the words "not true" in response to Obama's criticism of the Court's decision; see Linda Greenhouse, "Justice Alito's Reaction," *New York Times*, January 27, 2010, http://opinionator.blogs.nytimes.com/2010/01/27/justice-alitos-reaction/?_php=true&_type=blogs&_r=0 (last accessed April 24, 2014).

10 This is consistent with the conclusion of several scholars that several forces, including novelty, conflict, and geographic proximity affect newsworthiness (see Vining and Marcin 2014, 189).

11 There is an appreciable spike in the average number of sentences devoted to the majority opinion in the media's coverage of the October Term 1996. However, this appears to be anomalous, as the attention to the majority opinion returns to its prior levels in both the 2006 and 2009 terms.

12 We identified Court reporters using Spill and Oxley's list reported in their 2003 *Judicature* article and an email from the dean of the Supreme Court press corps, Lyle Denniston, who noted all the Court reporters he has worked with during his five-plus decades of covering the Court. We thank Lyle for his assistance with this project.

13 The trend holds for the "living constitution" justification as well. The difference is .15 (t = 5.16).

References

Baird, Vanessa A., and Amy Gangl. 2006. "Shattering the Myth of Legality: The Impact of the Media's Framing of Supreme Court Procedures on Perceptions of Fairness." *Political Psychology* 27 (4):597–614.

Bartels, Larry M. 1993. "Messages Received: The Political Impact of Media Exposure." *American Political Science Review* 87 (2):267–85.

Clawson, Rosalee A., Harry C. N. Strine IV, and Eric N. Waltenburg. 2003. "Framing Supreme Court Decisions: The Mainstream Versus the Black Press." *Journal of Black Studies* 33 (6):784–800.

Clawson, Rosalee A., and Eric N. Waltenburg. 2009. *Legacy and Legitimacy: Black Americans and the Supreme Court*. Philadelphia: Temple University Press.

Davis, Richard. 1994. *Decisions and Images: The Supreme Court and the Press*. Englewood Cliffs, NJ: Prentice-Hall.

Denniston, Lyle. n.d. "Lyle Denniston on Changing Media Coverage of the Supreme Court." C-SPAN. http://supremecourt.c-span.org/Video/Historians/SC_HIST_LyleD_06.aspx (last accessed August 10, 2013).

Franklin, Charles H., and Liane C. Kosaki. 1995. "Media, Knowledge, and Public Evaluations of the Supreme Court." In *Contemplating Courts*, pp. 352–376. ed. L. Epstein. Washington, DC: CQ Press.

Gibson, James L., and Gregory A. Caldeira. 2009. *Citizens, Courts, and Confirmations: Positivity Theory and the Judgments of the American People*. Princeton, NJ: Princeton University Press.

56 The Decisional Myth

———. 2011. "Has Legal Realism Damaged the Legitimacy of the U.S. Supreme Court?" *Law and Society Review* 45 (1):195–219.

Gibson, James L., Milton Lodge, and Benjamin Woodson. 2012. "The Symbols of Legitimacy: Thinking, Fast and Slow, About the U.S. Supreme Court." In *Annual Meeting of the American Political Science Association*. New Orleans.

Johnston, Christopher D., and Brandon L. Bartels. 2010. "Sensationalism and Sobriety: Differential Media Exposure and Attitudes Toward American Courts." *Public Opinion Quarterly* 74 (2):260–86.

LaRowe, Nicholas, and Valerie Hoekstra. 2014. "On and Off the Supreme Court Beat: Differences in Newspaper Coverage of the Supreme Court and Implications for Public Support." In *Covering the United States Supreme Court in the Digital Age*, pp. 126–152. ed. R. Davis. New York: Cambridge University Press.

McCombs, Maxwell. 2005. "The Agenda-Setting Function of the Press." In *The Press*, pp. 156–168. ed. G. Overholser and K. H. Jamieson. New York: Oxford University Press.

Scheb, John M., and William Lyons. 2001. "Judicial Behavior and Public Opinion: Popular Expectations Regarding the Factors that Influence Supreme Court Decisions." *Political Behavior* 23 (2):181–94.

Segal, Jeffrey A., Lee Epstein, Charles M. Cameron, and Harold J. Spaeth. 1995. "Ideological Values and the Votes of U.S. Supreme Court Justices Revisited." *Journal of Politics* 57 (3):812–23.

Shanto, Iyenger, Mark D. Peters, and Donald R. Kinder. 1982. "Experimental Demonstrations of the 'Not-So-Minimal' Consequences of Television News Programs." *American Political Science Review* 74 (4):848–58.

Spill, Rorie L., and Zoe M. Oxley. 2003. "Philosopher Kings or Political Actors: How the Media Portray the Supreme Court." *Judicature* 87 (1):23–29.

Strickler, Richard James. 2014. "The Supreme Court and New Media Technologies." In *Covering the United States Supreme Court in the Digital Age*, pp. 61–88. ed. R. Davis. New York: Cambridge University Press.

Vining, Jr., Richard L., and Phil Marcin. 2014. "Explaining Intermedia Coverage of Supreme Court Decisions." In *Covering the United States Supreme Court in the Digital Age*, pp. 89–108. ed. R. Davis. New York: Cambridge University Press.

4

THE DECISIONAL MYTH, PART 2—THE LANDMARK CASES

In this chapter, we continue to explore the "cult of personality" by focusing on the oversaturation of the Court's docket found in chapter 3. Here, we analyze the coverage of the Court's docket in terms of the media's treatment of those cases that have been identified as "landmark rulings" rather than by issue areas. The key question is how might the public's image of the Court be affected by media coverage of both types of cases when they are highly salient (politically, legally, or both)? Since landmark cases tend to deal with profound social and legal issues, oversaturation on these issues may lead to a more realistic representation of the Court's work. However, if the coverage of landmark cases is skewed toward the politically charged case, regardless of its legal implications, the image of the Court may be distorted, as we found in chapters 2 and 3, as will be the public's perception of the Court's work. In this chapter, we begin with an examination of landmark cases as a whole, describing overall differences within this subset of cases compared to the other cases on the Court's decisional docket that the media covered, but that were not necessarily recognized by history as seminal. We then focus more narrowly on the coverage of the landmark cases for each term—the issue areas highlighted and the major decisions that garner media attention. We end each of these separate analyses with a comparison between the landmark cases and the non-landmark cases covered in that term, specifically focusing on which cases serve as "news pegs,"[1] to tease out any additional significant differences in coverage of these major cases.

In terms of identifying salient cases, there are two main metrics. Often scholars will simply utilize the paper of record, the *New York Times*, and note whether a case appears on its front page (Epstein and Segal 2000). Given the paper's reputation and our prior analyses that show that the *New York Times* simply covers more

58 The Landmark Cases

than its competition in relation to the Supreme Court, this measure makes perfect sense. However, for our purposes it would be a tautological indicator. Simply put, we cannot use the *New York Times* to identify each term's most salient cases and then profoundly note that the *New York Times* was the best at covering such cases. Therefore, we turn to the second common metric—whether the case makes the *Congressional Quarterly* list of historic or landmark cases. The latest listing appearing in the *Guide to the U.S. Supreme Court* ends with the October Term 2009. Therefore, the fifth edition of the *Guide*, as identified and compiled by *Los Angeles Times* Court reporter David Savage, serves to identify landmark cases for our analysis in this chapter.

Savage and his predecessors identify a total of 51 landmark cases in the six terms under study. This resource covers our entire time period; however, Savage only identifies two cases as landmark from the October Term 2009. Table 4.1 reproduces the list along with a general indication of the substance of each case.

The data contained in Table 4.1 is daunting in terms of press coverage when you consider that landmark status is somewhat of a post-hoc assessment, often coming after the close of a term or even after several years when more perspective is available. Yet, the members of the press must determine, in the moment, which, if any, cases deserve significant amounts of coverage. Given that many of these landmark cases met the high threshold of "news peg" status for one or more of our media outlets, it seems clear that the media are doing a good job identifying cases of import. Indeed, as we show in Table 4.2, with the exception of the 2006 Term, at least one of our sources covered every landmark case to some degree. The convergence of the media with respect to coverage of landmark cases is consistent with prior studies showing that the media tend to cohere around "the most salient events" (see Vining and Marcin 2014, 186).

It bears mentioning that staff reporters are as likely to author stories about the landmark cases as are Court reporters. Court reporters are responsible for almost 58% of the stories covering non-landmark cases; whereas, these same reporters' bylines only appear on 40% of the landmark stories—equal to the 40% of stories on landmark decisions attributed to staff reporters. These statistics support the conclusion that landmark cases indeed are often news pegs, or at least deemed worthy of more than one story, and so the reporting of these cases diffuses beyond the small coterie of elite Court reporters. Perhaps more interesting is that over the five terms included in this analysis, the landmark stories in the later terms (1996 and 2006) comprise a larger proportion of the total number of stories. Thus, these especially salient cases—legally, politically, or both—are attracting the bulk of the media's attention by the end of our time period.

When we turn to an exploration of the content of these stories, we find that they tend to provide more information about the Court's decision. Across the total time series, stories on landmark cases averaged more than six sentences reporting on the majority opinion, while non-landmark cases average just a tick

TABLE 4.1 CQ Landmark Cases

Case Name	Citation	Term	Vote	Majority Opinion Author	Substance	Total Number of Stories	News Peg?
Michelin Tire Corp. v. Wages	423 U.S. 276	1975	8–0	Brennan	Import/Export Clause	6	Yes
Buckley v. Valeo	424 U.S. 1	1975	8–0; 7–1; 6–2	Unsigned	First Amendment / speech	71	Yes
Washington v. Davis	426 U.S. 229	1975	7–2	White	Equal Protection Clause	4	No
Nat. League of Cities v. Usery	426 U.S. 833	1975	5–4	Rehnquist	Tenth Amendment	11	Yes
Runyon v. McCrary, Fairfax-Brewster Sch., Inc. v. Gonzales, S. Indep. Sch. Ass'n Inc. v. Gonzales, S. Indep. Sch. Ass'n v. McCrary	427 U.S. 160	1975	7–2	Stewart	Civil Rights Act	7	No
Elrod v. Burns	427 U.S. 347	1975	5–3	Brennan	First Amendment / speech	5	No
Pasadena City Bd. of Educ. v. Spangler	427 U.S. 424	1975	6–2	Rehnquist	Equal Protection Clause	10	Yes
Neb. Press Ass'n v. Stuart	427 U.S. 539	1975	9–0	Burger	First Amendment / press	11	No
Gregg v. Georgia; Proffitt v. Florida; Jurek v. Texas	428 U.S. 153, 242, 262	1975	7–2	Stewart (Stevens, Powell)	Eighth Amendment / death penalty	17,2,4	Yes
Woodson v. North Carolina, Roberts v. Louisiana	428 U.S. 280, 325	1975	5–4	Stewart (Stevens)	Eighth Amendment / death penalty	9,6	Yes
Stone v. Powell, Wolff v. Rice	428 U.S. 465	1975	6–3	Powell	Habeas corpus	3	No
Vasquez v. Hillery	474 U.S. 254	1985	6–3	Marshall	Equal Protection Clause	1	No
Batson v. Kentucky	476 U.S. 79	1985	7–2	Powell	Sixth & Fourteenth Amendments	6	No
Lockhart v. McCree	476 U.S. 162	1985	6–3	Rehnquist	Sixth Amendment	6	No
Wygant v. Jackson Bd. of Educ.	476 U.S. 267	1985	5–4	Powell	Affirmative action	14	Yes

(Continued)

TABLE 4.1 (Continued)

Case Name	Citation	Term	Vote	Majority Opinion Author	Substance	Total Number of Stories	News Peg?
Thornburgh v. Am. Coll. of Obstetricians & Gynecologists	476 U.S. 747	1985	5–4	Blackmun	Abortion	12	Yes
Ford v. Wainwright	477 U.S. 399	1985	5–4	Marshall	Eighth Amendment / death penalty	4	No
Davis v. Bandemer	478 U.S. 109	1985	6–3; 7–2	White	Equal Protection Clause	7	Yes
Bowers v. Hardwick	478 U.S. 186	1985	5–4	White	Right to privacy	11	Yes
Local 28 of the Sheet Metal Workers Int'l Ass'n v. EEOC	478 U.S. 421	1985	5–4	Brennan	Affirmative action	11	Yes
Local 93 of Int'l Ass'n of Firefighters v. City of Cleveland	478 U.S. 501	1985	6–3	Brennan	Affirmative action	15	Yes
Bowsher v. Synar, Senate v. Synar, O'Neill v. Synar	478 U.S. 714	1985	7–2	Burger	Separation of powers	14	Yes
Emp't Div., Dep't of Human Res. of Or. v. Smith	494 U.S. 872	1989	5–4	Scalia	First Amendment / religion	12	Yes
Bd. of Educ. of the Westside Cmty. Schs. (Dist. 66) v. Mergens	496 U.S. 226	1989	8–1	O'Connor	First Amendment / establishment	10	Yes
United States v. Eichmann; United States v. Haggerty	496 U.S. 310	1989	5–4	Brennan	First Amendment / speech	26	Yes
Mich. Dep't of State Police v. Sitz	496 U.S. 444	1989	6–3	Rehnquist	Fourth Amendment / search & seizure	10	No
Rutan v. Republican Party of Ill., Frech v. Rutan	497 U.S. 62	1989	5–4	Brennan	First Amendment / speech	11	No
Cruzan v. Dir., Mo. Dep't of Health	497 U.S. 261	1989	5–4	Rehnquist	Right to privacy	14	Yes
Hodgson v. Minnesota, Minnesota v. Hodgson	497 U.S. 417	1989	5–4, 5–4	Stevens	Abortion	7	No
Metro Broad. Inc. v. FCC, Astroline Commc'ns Co. v. Shurberg Broad. of Hartford	497 U.S. 547	1989	5–4	Brennan	Affirmative action	7	No

TABLE 4.1 (Continued)

Case Name	Citation	Term	Vote	Majority Opinion Author	Substance	Total Number of Stories	News Peg?
Ohio v. Akron Ctr. for Reprod. Health	497 U.S. 502	1989	6–3	Kennedy	Abortion	4	No
Turner Broad. Sys. v. FCC	520 U.S. 180	1996	5–4	Kennedy	First Amendment / speech	6	No
Clinton v. Jones	520 U.S. 681	1996	9–0	Stevens	Presidential immunity	18	Yes
Printz v. United States	521 U.S. 898	1996	5–4	Scalia	Federalism	9	Yes
Agostini v. Felton	521 U.S. 203	1996	5–4	O'Connor	First Amendment / establishment	6	No
Kansas v. Hendricks	521 U.S. 346	1996	5–4	Thomas	Double jeopardy	3	No
City of Boerne v. Flores	521 U.S. 507	1996	6–3	Kennedy	Congressional power	9	Yes
Amchem Prods., Inc. v. Windsor	521 U.S. 591	1996	6–2	Ginsburg	Asbestos litigation	3	No
United States v. O'Hagan	521 U.S. 642	1996	6–3	Ginsburg	SEC rules	3	No
Washington v. Glucksberg	521 U.S. 702	1996	9–0	Rehnquist	Right to privacy	15	Yes
Vaco v. Quill	521 U.S. 793	1996	9–0	Rehnquist	Right to privacy	10	Yes
Reno v. ACLU	521 U.S. 844	1996	9–0	Stevens	First Amendment / speech	12	No
Massachusetts v. EPA	549 U.S. 497	2006	5–4	Stevens	Clean Air Act	20	Yes
Gonzales v. Carhart	550 U.S. 124	2006	5–4	Kennedy	Abortion	34	Yes
Ledbetter v. Goodyear Tire & Rubber Co.	550 U.S. 618	2006	5–4	Alito	Title VII	12	No
Leegin Creative Leather Prods. v. PSKS	551 U.S. 877	2006	5–4	Kennedy	Sherman Antitrust Act	4	No
Morse v. Frederick	551 U.S. 393	2006	6–3	Roberts	First Amendment / speech	8	No
FEC v. Wis. Right to Life, Inc.	551 U.S. 449	2006	5–4	Roberts	First Amendment / speech	10	No
Parents Involved in Cmty. Schs. v. Seattle Sch. Dist. No. 1	551 U.S. 701	2006	5–4	Roberts	Affirmative action	13	Yes
Citizens United v. FEC	558 U.S. 310	2009	5–4	Kennedy	First Amendment / speech	32	Yes
United States v. Stevens	559 U.S. 460	2009	8–1	Roberts	First Amendment / speech	7	No

TABLE 4.2 Frequency of Media Coverage of Landmark Cases

	New York Times	Washington Post	Los Angeles Times	CBS	Total Media
1975					
Unique cases	120	94	64	32	310
Unique landmark	13	8	12	7	13
1985					
Unique cases	71	90	75	25	261
Unique landmark	9	10	10	8	11
1989					
Unique cases	90	39	69	21	219
Unique landmark	9	4	9	8	9
1996					
Unique cases	52	35	12	14	126
Unique landmark	2	10	6	5	10
2006					
Unique cases	39	26	29	8	102
Unique landmark	6	5	6	4	6

*October Term 2009 excluded due to incomplete list of landmark cases.

	New York Times	Washington Post	Los Angeles Times	CBS	Total Media
1975					
Non-landmark stories	203 (83%)	141 (90%)	73 (73%)	36 (75%)	453 (83%)
Landmark stories	41 (17%)	15 (10%)	12 (25%)	27 (27%)	95 (17%)
1985					
Non-landmark stories	67 (73%)	89 (66%)	95 (81%)	17 (68%)	268 (77%)
Landmark stories	25 (27%)	45 (34%)	23 (19%)	23 (32%)	101 (27%)
1989					
Non-landmark stories	145 (82%)	38 (81%)	128 (72%)	15 (58%)	326 (76%)
Landmark stories	32 (18%)	9 (19%)	49 (28%)	11 (42%)	101 (24%)
1996					
Non-landmark stories	27 (87%)	34 (36%)	7 (25%)	9 (50%)	77 (45%)
Landmark stories	4 (13%)	60 (64%)	21 (75%)	9 (50%)	94 (55%)
2006					
Non-landmark stories	50 (53%)	28 (60%)	28 (48%)	3 (30%)	109 (52%)
Landmark stories	45 (47%)	19 (40%)	30 (52%)	7 (70%)	101 (48%)

below four ($|t| = 3.88$; $p \leq 0.00$).[2] This tendency is particularly true in the earlier terms. Accordingly, in the October Term 1975, the average number of sentences reporting the majority opinion of a case is 3.95; for landmark cases this average rises to 7.32 ($|t| = 2.49$; $p \leq 0.01$). A similar pattern holds for the 1985 Term. Non-landmark cases average 3.39 sentences reporting on the majority opinion. For landmark cases, the average number of sentences soars to 8.41 ($|t| = 2.92$; $p \leq 0.00$). In every case, these significant differences have effect sizes greater than .2, that is, greater than a small or marginal difference in the means (see Cohen 1992, 157). By the end of our time series, however, the attention the media devotes to the majority opinion in landmark cases is not statistically distinguishable from the attention our media outlets devote to the other cases they cover. Thus, in the 1996 Term, coverage of the majority opinion in landmark cases averaged 6.07 sentences; the majority opinion in non-landmark cases, 5.4 ($|t| = .57$; $p \leq 0.57$). In the 2006 Term, the comparators are 4.23 and 3.58 ($|t| = 1.23$; $p \leq 0.22$). In terms of covering the facts of the case, stories on landmark decisions actually average slightly fewer sentences than do the stories on the non-landmark decisions—a difference that achieves statistical significance ($|t| = 2.23$; $p \leq 0.03$). The effect size, however, barely registers (0.11). When reporting on the votes, stories on landmark cases again provide greater coverage (2.51 sentences versus 1.93; $|t| = 5.65$; $p \leq 0.00$). Here, the effect size is a more robust 0.41. In the end, however, perhaps the most consequential differences are in the total sentences per story, although the difference in the amount of coverage between the two types of decisions is by no means consistent across our time series. Table 4.3 reports these comparisons.

In Table 4.1, we provided more detail on the issue areas of these cases. Rather than simply note that a case dealt with criminal procedure writ large, for example, we described it as an Eighth Amendment death penalty case. We now return to Spaeth's coarser issue areas as our backdrop. In chapter 3, we spent considerable time discussing the tendency of the media to overreport or saturate certain issue areas (see also Vining and Marcin 2014). We would expect this trend to continue in the subset of landmark cases, given the documented salience of these cases. Our expectations were met. In five of the six terms (1975, 1985,

TABLE 4.3 Mean Sentences per Story: Landmark vs. Non-Landmark Decisions*

Term	1975	1985	1989	1996	2006
Mean Total Sentences: Landmark	37.36	35.3	35.54	37	41.74
Mean Total Sentences: Non-Landmark	24.38	24.4	34.95	29.34	42.66
$|t|$	5.02	4.24	0.23	2.92	0.23
$p \leq$	0.00	0.00	0.82	0.00	0.82
Effect Size	0.65	0.70	0.03	0.45	0.03

*October Term 2009 excluded due to incomplete list of landmark cases.

64 The Landmark Cases

1989, 2006, and 2009), either First Amendment or civil rights landmark cases are reported most frequently. For 1985, 1989, and 1996, cases centering on the right to privacy take second place; in the October Term 2006, privacy landmark cases move into the top slot. The media's emphasis on privacy decisions is not unique to the 2006 Term; indeed, in all terms but 1975 and 2009, privacy landmark cases do not constitute less than 20% of the total stories covering this subset of cases.[3]

Recall that in chapter 3 we found that Court reporters are more likely to include legal justifications for decisions in their stories than are staff and wire correspondents. Taking this information, and combining it with the findings here—that landmark cases serve as vehicles for the saturation of an issue (particularly First Amendment and civil rights) and are often covered by staff reporters—it is likely that, in relative terms, readers are more often exposed to the "cult of personality" myth in coverage of landmark decisions. The dynamic works something like this: the Court reporter discusses the decision itself and its legal justifications, while later stories—stories more often written by staff reporters—follow normal journalistic tendencies to include more coverage on the personal and political. We now turn to a detailed discussion of the content of the media's coverage of the landmark decisions handed down during our time series.

October Term 1975

During the October Term 1975, there were 15 distinct landmark decisions.[4] The issue area from this term that received the most coverage is the First Amendment. The saturation of First Amendment coverage, however, is mostly due to *Buckley v. Valeo* (424 U.S. 1 [1976]). Simply put, the *Buckley* ruling and the subsequent political budget battles kept the Court and its decision in the news. Seventy-one of the 87 stories in the First Amendment category and 52% of the coverage of all the landmark cases from this term refer to this one case.

Was *Buckley* unusual? Did the media converge on any other landmark cases handed down in the 1975 Term like a school of piranha in a feeding frenzy? Not really. Let us turn to the seven landmark criminal procedure cases for comparison. The coverage here is somewhat surprising given that these seven cases were announced in groups with the three major challenges to the states' new death penalty procedures coming in *Gregg v. Georgia, Proffit v. Florida*, and *Jurek v. Texas* (428 U.S. 153, 242, and 262 [1976]). In each case, the Court examined the new state laws to determine if the states complied with its directives from *Furman v. Georgia* (408 U.S. 238 [1972]) to alleviate the flaws in death penalty due process. And, in these cases, the Court agreed that the states did make the process fair and that capital punishment does not, on its own, violate the prohibition against cruel and unusual punishment found in the Eighth Amendment. Similarly *Woodson v.*

North Carolina and *Roberts v. Louisiana* (428 U.S. 280, 325 [1976]) were coupled together, as both announced the Court's stand on mandatory capital sentences. Noting that such sentences "depart markedly from contemporary standards," the Court struck them down. Finally, in *Stone v. Powell* and *Wolff v. Rice* (428 U.S. 465 [1976]), the Court addressed whether a federal court could deny habeas corpus relief. These decisions continued the Court's departure from viewing the exclusionary rule as a constitutional mandate and here, as elsewhere, they ruled that applying the rule when it did not serve as a deterrent against police misconduct was not required. Since there was a full and fair airing of the Fourth Amendment issue in both cases and no additional deterrent effect would accrue, the justices held the lower court could deny the writ. These three rulings and seven cases were covered in 41 stories.

The other landmark decisions handed down in the 1975 Term did not generate nearly the cascade effect of the First Amendment or criminal procedure cases despite their import, although *National League of Cities v. Usery, Pasadena v. Spangler,* and *Nebraska Press Ass'n v. Stuart* were covered in 11, 10, and 11 stories, respectively across all four media outlets. *National League of Cities* (426 U.S. 833 [1976]) limited congressional power vis-à-vis the states. Congress included state employees in its labor regulations and the states balked. William Rehnquist, writing for the Court, previewed one of the major issue areas he would champion while chief justice: preserving state authority and autonomy. Here, with a marginal majority, Rehnquist curbed Congress, noting that the federal government cannot dictate how the states pay their employees. In *Pasadena City Board of Education v. Spangler* (427 U.S. 424 [1976]), Rehnquist, again speaking for the Court, relieved Pasadena of a court order to rearrange its attendance zones yearly to keep up with changes in population. The Court held that natural population movement does not violate the precedent set in *Brown v. Board of Education* (347 U.S. 483 [1954]). In some sense, it is shocking that *Nebraska Press Ass'n v. Stuart* (427 U.S. 539 [1976]) did not receive more coverage—it did not even achieve news peg status—as the case directly affected media access to courtrooms. The Court, with Chief Justice Burger writing, chastised trial judges for closing a courtroom or restraining the press too quickly.

When we examine the media's coverage of the non-landmark cases in the 1975 Term, we see a similar pattern of saturation. The First Amendment, civil rights, and criminal procedure are the foci of media coverage. It is important to note, however, that the issue area, not the definitive or potential import of the case, garnered the media's attention. To be sure, the press certainly recognized some of the landmark cases as especially salient; many were covered in four or more stories. The average frequency of coverage per case over the entire dataset is one story. Those landmark decisions that did not receive heightened attention tended to be companion cases like *Proffitt* (two stories) compared to 17 stories for *Gregg*.

66 The Landmark Cases

News Pegs

To further emphasize this point, we explore the media's treatment of landmark decisions in terms of "news pegs." In chapter 2, we introduced the concept of a news peg (see Clawson et al. 2003). A news peg is cascading coverage; one story becomes many for some issues, cases, or events. Here we use both the standard deviation and the arithmetic mean of stories per case for each newspaper in each term. More specifically, the threshold for a decision to obtaining news peg status is if the number of stories covering that decision was at least 1.5 standard deviations greater than the relevant mean. By this measure, in the October Term 1975, there were two news pegs, one from the *New York Times* and one from the *Los Angeles Times*, *not* generated by a landmark cases. The *New York Times* gave a significant amount of coverage to *Carla A. Hills, Secretary of Housing and Urban Development v. Gautreaux* (425 U.S. 284 [1976])—a case involving discrimination in public housing. After this decision, there was widespread speculation in the media about where low-income housing would appear now that the federal government could no longer keep such projects within metropolitan boundaries. The *Los Angeles Times* pegged *United States v. Janis* (428 U.S. 433 [1976]). *Janis* was another criminal procedure case that revealed how far the Court was willing to go with its deterrence justification for the exclusionary rule. Here, the Court held that the Internal Revenue Service could use evidence illegally seized by state officials in a civil trial because the exclusion would serve no deterrent effect on the state officials, and the federal officials did not err.

The *New York Times* and the *Los Angeles Times* are not the only media outlets that found *Gautreaux* or *Janis* to be newsworthy. *Gautreaux* received coverage from all of our sources. In fact, CBS broadcast three individual stories on this discrimination decision. (In our news peg analysis in chapter 3, we did not include CBS because the overall number of stories it reported is so low—only 137 total across all six terms; it is likely, however, that this case would have stood out as a news peg for the broadcaster.) *Janis* made the pages of both the *Washington Post* and the *New York Times*. The number of stories in either paper did not, however, reach our news peg criterion.

October Term 1985

The *CQ Guide* identified 10 cases as landmarks for the October Term 1985, and these cases were covered in 101 news stories across our media outlets. In this term, civil rights cases comprised the bulk of the landmark rulings (53%), trailed by cases raising the issue of privacy (23%). Fourteen stories concerned cases coded as miscellaneous (14%), and 10 fell under the rubric of criminal procedure (10%). For this term, however, the broad category of civil rights can easily be replaced with a narrow one of affirmative action. During this term, the Court heard three affirmative action cases, all designated as landmark decisions. These three cases dominated the media's attention. They accounted for nearly 40% of all the news coverage of the landmark decisions and just over 10% of all coverage of the 1985 Term included in our dataset.

Only four of the landmark cases did not serve as news pegs during this term and all four of the cases fall under the rubric of criminal procedure and rights. In *Vasquez v. Hillery* (474 U.S. 254 [1986]) and *Batson v. Kentucky* (476 U.S. 79 [1986]), the Court heard challenges to the exclusion of minorities from a grand jury and petit jury, respectively. In both cases, the Court ruled that the exclusion violated the Constitution. The other two cases, *Lockhart v. McCree* (476 U.S. 162 [1986]) and *Ford v. Wainwright* (477 U.S. 399 [1986]) involved procedures related to the administration of the death penalty. In *Lockhart*, the Court determined that in a case where the death penalty is an option, there is no violation of the Sixth Amendment if the jurors are "death-qualified"—that is, jurors unwilling to apply the death penalty in any circumstances can be removed for cause. *Ford* challenged Florida's procedure for determining competency for the administration of the death penalty. Noting that the execution of the insane is cruel and unusual, Justice Marshall determined that Florida's procedures were so flawed as to run afoul of due process. It is somewhat shocking, given the primacy of criminal cases in most terms, that none of our papers concentrated coverage on one or more of these cases, particularly *Batson* and *Vasquez*, as these two cases merge criminal and civil rights issues.

News Pegs

Given their controversial nature, it is not at all surprising that all three affirmative action cases achieved news peg status for at least one of our media outlets. In *Wygant v. Jackson Board of Education* (476 U.S. 267 [1986]) (14 stories), traditional rules of seniority collided with an affirmative action plan. Under a collective bargaining agreement, the Jackson Board of Education agreed that if it had to lay off teachers, seniority would dictate who received pink slips, with the stipulation that the percentage of minority teachers must stay at the level attained at the time of the layoff. This "but if" clause meant that some white teachers with more seniority were laid off in favor of less senior minority teachers. The Court determined that the affirmative action plan practiced here violated the Equal Protection Clause. There was no finding that the Jackson Board of Education had practiced discrimination; therefore, the Board did not have a compelling justification for discriminating based upon race.

Affirmative action plans were narrowly upheld in *Local 28 of the Sheet Metal Workers International Ass'n v. EEOC* (478 U.S. 421 [1986]) (11 stories) and in *Local 93 of International Ass'n of Firefighters v. City of Cleveland* (478 U.S. 501 [1986]) (15 stories). In these cases, Justice Brennan stated for the Court that Title VII of

68 The Landmark Cases

the *Civil Rights Act* did not prohibit race-conscious quota programs created to remedy past discrimination, even if those benefiting did not face discrimination directly. Unlike in *Wygant*, there was a clear and compelling history of discrimination in union membership, hiring, and promotion.

Two additional cases round out the general civil rights category. They deal with discrimination in the selection of grand and petit juries—*Batson v. Kentucky* (476 U.S. 79 [1986]) (six stories) and *Vasquez v. Hillery* (474 U.S. 254 [1986]) (one story). Neither of these cases served as news pegs, suggesting that the public salience of affirmative action led to the extent of coverage for the civil rights issue area.

The issue area of privacy takes second place in this term due to two cases—the only two privacy cases on the docket in the 1975 Term. The first is *Bowers v. Hardwick* (478 U.S. 186 [1986]). In this case, Georgia's anti-sodomy law was challenged and sustained, and the Court began its journey through the choppy waters of the LGBT fight for equal rights. Determining that the constitutional right of privacy defined in *Griswold v. Connecticut* (381 U.S. 479 [1965]) did not extend to consensual sodomy, with Justice White noting that sodomy, consensual or not, is not "deeply rooted in this Nation's history and tradition." Justice Blackmun dissented, and in his opinion he quoted Justice Brandeis's dissent from *Olmstead v. United States* (277 U.S. 438 [1928]): the case "is about 'the most comprehensive of rights and the right most valued by civilized men,' namely, 'the right to be let alone.'" This dissent would be vindicated some 17 years later when the Court overturned *Bowers* in *Lawrence v. Texas* (539 U.S. 558 [2003]).

The second privacy case generated 12 stories (almost 12% of all the landmark stories). While *Thornburgh v. American College of Obstetricians and Gynecologists* (476 U.S. 747 [1986]) may not be one of the most prominent challenges to *Roe v. Wade* (410 U.S. 113 [1973]), it was one of the first cases to test the resolve of the Court on the then still new expansion of the right of privacy. Pennsylvania instituted a series of constraints on the ability of women to obtain and doctors to perform abortions. Like subsequent challenges, the state was testing how much leeway the tripartite test of *Roe* gave it in suppressing abortion rights. Among other regulations, the law required an informed consent, limited medical techniques that could be used in later term abortions, and required a second physician to be present for post-viability procedures. Justice Blackmun, reprising his role from *Roe*, wrote for the five-person majority. Balancing the right to privacy and concern for maternal health against the state's interest, the Court voided the Pennsylvania law.

The prominence of the miscellany category in this term makes a great deal of sense when we recognize that all 14 of those stories were generated from *Bowsher v. Synar*, *Senate v. Synar*, and *O'Neill v. Synar* (478 U.S. 714 [1986]). *Bowsher* found the Court in the center of the budget battles between Congress and the Executive. In 1985, in an attempt to control ballooning deficits, Congress passed the *Gramm-Rudman-Hollings Deficit Control Act*. The Act had a fail-safe for meeting deficit reduction goals; if the federal budget did not meet the targets set by the Act, the Comptroller General was authorized to institute across-the-board cuts to meet the targets. The Court, with Chief Justice Burger writing, deemed the *Deficit Control Act* unconstitutional because it provided the Comptroller General, a legislative officer, with executive authority. The political implications and salience of the case were clear. The Court voided a bipartisan solution to federal budget woes—designed by Congress and signed by President Ronald Reagan. This is a classic example of the Supreme Court curtailing a pragmatic solution due to fidelity to a strict notion of separation of powers.

Criminal procedure cases make up the largest proportion of stories (25%) in the subset of non-landmark cases, followed by civil rights and First Amendment decisions (18% and 16% respectively). Three cases in this subset were news pegs, as defined in chapter 3. All three cases were pegs for the *Los Angeles Times*; two of the cases were First Amendment cases, while the third dealt with civil rights. Additionally, the First Amendment cases had a local flavor for the *Los Angeles Times* (on the effect of geographic proximity on newsworthiness, see Vining and Marcin 2014, 189). Centering on a zoning fight in the state of Washington, *City of Renton v. Playtime Theatres* (475 U.S. 41 [1986]) found ordinances restricting the location of adult theaters, as long as the theaters are not completely banned, to be valid under the Court's "time, place, and manner" doctrine. *Press-Enterprise Co. v. Superior Court of California* (478 U.S. 1 [1986]) followed on the heels of the *Nebraska Press Ass'n* ruling that the press has the right of access, under the First Amendment, to preliminary hearings.

The last non-landmark news peg from this term did not take place in California or the Pacific Northwest; yet, the *Los Angeles Times* overreported the case. *Bowen, Secretary of Health and Human Services v. American Hospital Ass'n, et al.* (476 U.S. 610 [1986]) dealt with regulations promulgated under Section 504 of the *Rehabilitation Act* of 1973. The regulations followed upon a controversial case from Indiana where parents of an infant refused treatment to clear an obstruction from the baby's esophagus. The new interim rules provided, among other things, that a department official should receive "expedited access to records and facilities" when an official deemed it "necessary to protect the life or health of a handicapped individual."[5] Legal challenges followed while the department worked on finalizing their rules. These challenges led to nullification of the interim rules but did not affect the final rules.

As the rule-writing process progressed, another medical case, similar to the Indiana one, occurred in New York. Suit followed in the New York state court system, with an unrelated individual seeking a guardian ad litem for the child. As these court proceedings continued, the parents were successful upon appeal. During these proceedings, the Department of Health and Human Services (HHS) received a complaint, claiming that the baby was "being discriminatorily denied medically indicated treatment" (*Bowen*, 476 U.S. at 621). HHS requested the

70 The Landmark Cases

records from the hospital, but the hospital refused the department's request due to a lack of parental consent. HHS then brought suit under its authority to enforce Section 504's requirements that HHS be provide access to the medical records of handicapped individuals in order to ensure compliance. HHS lost in both the district and circuit courts. Upon appeal to the Supreme Court, Justice Stevens, joined by Justices Marshall, Blackmun, and Powell, noted the case "presented . . . is whether the four mandatory provisions of the Final Rules are authorized by 504" (476 U.S. at 626). Chief Justice Burger concurred in the judgment but offered no opinion, and Justice Rehnquist did not take part in the case.

Based upon this description of the case, we hypothesize that the *Los Angeles Times* overreported the *Bowen* decision due to the emotionally charged background of the case. While the Court simply dealt with the issue of the Secretary's interpretation of Section 504, the facts of the case deal with whether or not infants should receive life-saving treatment. As we note in chapter 5 (see also Solberg and Waltenburg 2014), by this term the pro-life and pro-choice sides of the privacy debate are entrenched and this case's story—although not explicitly about the right to privacy or abortion—slides easily into that debate. If we investigate the reporting on *Bowen* a bit further, we find that all four of our media outlets covered this fight over the breadth of the Secretary's powers. Multiple stories appear in both the *New York Times* and the *Washington Post*. In contrast, *City of Renton* was not covered in the "paper of record," although it made an appearance in the pages of the *Post* and on-air for CBS. *Press-Enterprise Co.* received minimal coverage in the *New York Times* and the *Washington Post* (one story in each). In the trenches, so to speak, the various Court and staff reporters, and their editors, have a baseline sense of newsworthiness; whether some cases become foci for news is a question answered differently by the various mediums.

October Term 1989

In the October Term 1989, there were 11 cases selected as landmarks; two of these cases were consolidated with another case and its decision, yielding nine landmark decisions. The two partner cases (the second of a paired set) did not, in the press's eyes, merit coverage. Therefore, our four media outlets produced 101 stories based on nine landmark decisions. Stories about cases later identified as significant cases occupied 24% of all the stories produced that term. In other words, the media is not ignoring these cases; however, they are not necessarily identifying them as significant contemporaneously. Only three of these cases served as news pegs, and all three newspapers agreed on only one case as a news peg or focus.

As in the previous terms, the landmark cases focused on four salient issue areas. First Amendment cases contributed the most stories (58%), followed by the right to privacy (25%), with criminal procedure and civil rights bringing up the rear (10% and 7%, respectively). If we look to a finer description of the cases, we find

The Landmark Cases **71**

that the First Amendment stories are defined broadly—some dealing with the free exercise of religion, others with the establishment of religion, and the remainder falling into an oleo category. The biggest subset of cases and stories were classified as "protest demonstrations" according to the *Supreme Court Database*. Almost 26% of the stories were on cases that fall into this category. In this category, however, resides but one landmark decision—*United States v. Eichmann* (496 U.S. 310 [1990]). *Eichmann* was, in some senses, part two of a larger story. In 1989, the Supreme Court heard *Texas v. Johnson* (491 U.S. 397 [1989]), ruling that flag desecration, in this instance flag burning, is clearly political expression and therefore protected by the First Amendment. As Justice Kennedy eloquently stated in his short concurrence:

> With all respect to those views, I do not believe the Constitution gives us the right to rule as the dissenting Members of the Court urge, however painful this judgment is to announce. Though symbols often are what we ourselves make of them, the flag is constant in expressing beliefs Americans share, beliefs in law and peace and that freedom which sustains the human spirit. The case here today forces recognition of the costs to which those beliefs commit us. It is poignant but fundamental that the flag protects those who hold it in contempt.
>
> For all the record shows, this respondent was not a philosopher and perhaps did not even possess the ability to comprehend how repellent his statements must be to the Republic itself. But whether or not he could appreciate the enormity of the offense he gave, the fact remains that his acts were speech, in both the technical and the fundamental meaning of the Constitution. So I agree with the Court that he must go free. (491 U.S. at 421)

The decision propelled the issue onto the public and presidential agenda. Gallup surveyed the public immediately after this decision and a full 71% supported "a constitutional amendment to make flag burning illegal." (Support for an amendment remained above 60% until the turn of the century.)[6] In essence, the decision in *Johnson* dragged the Court into bare-knuckle politics as politicians sought to make hay off this emotionally charged issue. After the *Johnson* decision, Congress kept the issue going through the next election cycle and followed up with national legislation to protect the flag. In other words, this is probably an example of politicians recognizing a valence issue when they see one and seeking to use it for political gain. Given the nature of the bully pulpit, it is not surprising that the media would cover the story, and reporting that emphasized "the cult of personality" was a collateral effect.

Congress reacted quickly to *Johnson* and passed the *Flag Protection Act*, amending the 1968 *Flag Desecration Law* (18 U.S.C. § 700) in an effort to preempt a

72 The Landmark Cases

constitutional challenge and conform to the Court's decision in *Texas v. Johnson*. Although the original act was not challenged, it seems likely that the 1968 law would not survive an appearance before the Court. Indeed, the Court had issued a string of decisions providing protection for various forms of expression using the flag (verbal disparagement: *Street v. New York* (394 U.S. 576 [1969]); placing the flag onto clothing (here, the seat of the pants): *Smith v. Goguen* (415 U.S. 94 [1974]); and altering the flag with tape: *Spence v. Washington* (418 U.S. 405 [1974]). Congress hoped to inoculate the Act against a First Amendment challenge by removing language related to the content of speech against the flag and simply prohibited purposeful mutilation, defacement, defilement, burning, or trampling the flag.

The *Flag Protection Act* was challenged after the United States prosecuted under the statute twice (in the state of Washington and in the District of Columbia). After losing in district court, the United States appealed directly to the Supreme Court and again lost as the majority of justices viewed the Act as directly suppressing expression in violation of the First Amendment.

The other First Amendment cases all hovered around the same percentage— 12%, 11%, and 10%, respectively. They concerned the free exercise of religion, a miscellany category (which for our purposes can be identified as political speech), and "parochiaid." The free exercise case, in retrospect, is duly admitted to the ranks of the landmark cases. *Employment Division, Department of Human Resources of Oregon v. Smith* (494 U.S. 872 [1990]) somewhat ironically concerned two drug rehabilitation counselors who were fired because they ingested peyote during a religious ceremony. They sued to obtain their unemployment compensation but were denied because they were fired for misconduct. The counselors challenged the decision as burdening their free exercise of religion. The Court disagreed, determining that there was no violation of the free exercise of religion under the First Amendment by the denial of benefits. The counselors violated a law that incidentally infringed on their religious practice and there is no constitutional requirement to create exemptions to generally based criminal law for religious rites. This case serves as turning point in free exercise jurisprudence as the Court applied the belief versus action test, rather than strict scrutiny, marking a distinct deviation from precedent.

Although the *Smith* decision seemed less friendly to religion, the Court's second religion case, coming under the Establishment Clause, took a bit of mortar out of the wall separating church and state. In *Board of Education of the Westside Community Schools (District 66) v. Mergens* (496 U.S. 226 [1990]), the "parochiaid" case, a school denied a religious student club accommodations for meeting after school. The school argued that providing the space and other privileges to a religious student group would be supporting religion and contravening the Constitution. Eight of the justices disagreed and determined that the district cannot, under the Establishment Clause or the *Equal Access Act*, deny space or the use of facilities to a club based upon the content of its speech—religious or otherwise. In the majority's view, there was no support of religion. The school was not giving credit for membership or attendance, and there was no connection to classroom curriculum. The justices held that this group, though religious in substance, is equivalent to other similarly situated student groups and must be treated as such.

The last First Amendment case is a throwback to the days of machine politics and reciprocity for party loyalty. *Rutan v. Republican Party of Illinois*, decided along with *Frech v. Rutan* (497 U.S. 62 [1990]), challenged the policies of then Governor James Thompson. Thompson froze hiring in the state bureaucracy and only allowed the filling of vacancies, recalling workers from layoff, or creation of new positions if approved by his office. The system, it was charged, was essentially a means for political patronage, as participation in Republican primaries, donations to GOP candidates, and recommendations from other Republican officials in the state became necessary for successful applicants. Ruling against the governor, Justice Brennan wrote, "[t]o the victor belong only those spoils that may be constitutionally obtained" (497 U.S. at 62). And so, the Court ruled that hiring, like firing, could not be based upon a litmus test of party loyalty or support.

The 25 stories covering right-to-privacy cases include two abortion cases and one of the first tests of the right to die—*Cruzan v. Director, Missouri Department of Health* (497 U.S. 261 [1990]). Here, the Court held that the right to refuse medical treatment did not extend to incompetent persons unable to exercise the right. Unless "clear and convincing evidence" that a patient would not want continued medical care existed, the state could constitutionally favor life. Nancy Cruzan's parents wished to discontinue intravenous fluids and nutrition after a catastrophic car accident left their daughter in a persistent vegetative state. According to the lower courts, the Cruzans could not surpass the level of proof required by the Missouri courts to discontinue life support. A minimal majority agreed that Missouri and its courts did not err by using the "clear and convincing standard." Justice O'Connor concurred and suggested that deathbed legal battles could be avoided if individuals wishing to avoid extraordinary measures to maintain life in an emergency situation drafted a living will.

Both abortion cases, like *Thornburgh* earlier, tested the limits of state power under *Roe*. In *Hodgson v. Minnesota* and *Minnesota v. Hodgson* (497 U.S 417 [1990]), perhaps foretelling doctrinal changes to come, the Court narrowly ruled that Minnesota's parental notification law was unconstitutional. Minnesota passed a law requiring that both parents be notified prior to a minor obtaining an abortion and that after this notification, the minor must wait 48 hours before the procedure. To the majority, the dual notification was a burden that did not further the state's legitimate interests in protecting minors and ensuring that the minor was knowledgeable and the abortion was undertaken voluntarily. Consent from one parent would serve the same purposes. Conversely, the 48-hour waiting period after single-parent notification did further the state's interests. Later in the same

74 The Landmark Cases

term, the Court upheld Ohio's parental consent law in *Ohio v. Akron Center for Reproductive Health* (497 U.S. 502 [1990]). The Ohio law had a judicial bypass procedure for minors who wished to avoid informing a parent. A minor could prove maturity by going before a judge. However, the Ohio law also required the doctor to inform a parent of the procedure and the Court determined that medical notification could "assist the parent in approaching the problem in a mature and balanced way" (497 U.S. at 504).

The last 17 stories in this subset of cases for the October Term 1989 covered one search and seizure case (10 stories) and one affirmative action case (seven stories). *Michigan Department of State Police v. Sitz* (496 U.S. 444 [1990]) tested the constitutionality of highway sobriety checkpoints. Challenged as suspicionless searches under the Fourth Amendment, and thus unconstitutional, the Court held that balancing the minimal intrusion on motorists against the weight of the drunk-driving problem and its cost in lives, the state's interest easily prevails. There is no Fourth Amendment violation.

Metro Broadcasting Inc. v. FCC, combined with *Astroline Communications Co. v. Shurberg Broadcasting of Hartford, Inc.* (497 U.S. 547 [1990]), followed upon the heels of the major affirmative action cases from the 1985 Term. The petitioners challenged a federal policy that allowed preferences for minorities in the granting of broadcast licenses and, where broadcasters were in danger of losing their license, they could sell to a minority buyer before the FCC's final ruling on the station's viability. Justice Brennan announced the policies as constitutional remedial action that suited legislative goals. Broadcast program diversity is a national goal that serves all, not just minorities, and aligns with the First Amendment.

News Pegs

United States v. Eichmann is the only case on which all three newspapers concurred and drenched their audience in coverage of this case. In terms of landmark cases, very few from this term served as news pegs in general. The *New York Times* only pegged *Eichmann*; the *Washington Post* concentrated coverage on *Eichmann* and *Cruzan*; the *Los Angeles Times* pegged *Eichmann*, *Westside Community Schools*, and *Oregon v. Smith*.

As in previous terms, issues of criminal procedure still get the most coverage, eating up 33% of the stories among non-landmark cases. Judicial power, economic activity, and the First Amendment are the only other issue areas that receive 10% or more of the total coverage (15%, 14%, and 13%, respectively). Of the 326 non-landmark cases from this term, six cases served as news pegs and there was no overlap among the newspapers. The *Los Angeles Times* again chose to significantly overreport three cases, the *New York Times* found two cases worthy of such treatment, and the *Post* only pegged one.

The Landmark Cases **75**

For the *Los Angeles Times*, one of the cases was a First Amendment case and was homegrown. *Jimmy Swaggart Ministries v. Board of Equalization of California* (493 U.S. 378 [1990]) determined that the state of California did not violate either the Free Exercise Clause or the Establishment Clause of the First Amendment by taxing the sale of religious items. *Osborne v. Ohio* (495 U.S. 103 [1990]) skates the fine line between the First Amendment and the right to privacy but in the end is a criminal procedure case. Osborne was convicted of possession of child pornography and challenged the state law as a violation of his right to receive information as per *Stanley v. Georgia* (394 U.S. 557 [1969]); he made several due process arguments as well. The Court disagreed, finding that Ohio could criminalize the possession of child pornography and that the law was not vague or overbroad. Still, a new trial was ordered because the Court determined that the jury instructions on lewdness were faulty. The last case from the *Los Angeles Times*—*United States v. Verdugo-Urquidez* (494 U.S. 259 [1990])—was also a criminal procedure case where the Court determined that the Search and Seizure Clause of the Fourth Amendment did not apply to property owned by absent nonresident aliens; the protections only apply to the people "who are part of a national community or who have otherwise developed sufficient connection within this country to be considered part of that community" (494 U.S. at 265).

The only non-landmark case the *Washington Post* significantly overreported was also a criminal procedure case. This is not terribly surprising given the salience of these cases and the sheer number of them given coverage. In *Butler v. Kenneth D. McKellar, Warden et al.* (494 U.S. 407 [1990]), Butler invoked his Fifth Amendment rights when interrogated about an assault and battery charge. He received and was represented by his lawyer. Later he was questioned about a different charge: murder. This time Butler waived his right and confessed. During the October Term 1987, the Court announced a new rule that a request for an attorney extends to questioning in a separate investigation (*Arizona v. Roberson*, 486 U.S. 675 [1988]), and Butler argued that the new rule applied to his situation; thus, his Fifth Amendment right was violated. The justices disagreed, noting that the new rule announced in *Roberson* did not automatically apply retroactively.

In contrast, both cases highlighted by the "paper of record," the *New York Times*, were civil rights cases with a bit of judicial powers added to the mix. In *Missouri v. Jenkins* (495 U.S. 33 [1990]), a district court judge, finding that the Kansas City, Missouri, schools were still segregated, imposed a tax to pay for remedial measures. *Spallone v. United States* (493 U.S. 265 [1990]) continued a Title VII battle that began in Yonkers, New York. Earlier, a court found that Yonkers had intentionally discriminated in its public housing. After a failed appeal, the city agreed to a consent decree but then stalled implementation. At this point, a district court ordered implementation and held that failure to comply would result in contempt charges and escalating fines. When the city council defeated a resolution

76 The Landmark Cases

of intent regarding the implementation of the consent decree, the judge imposed contempt charges and fines on both the city and the council members. In both *Jenkins* and *Spallone*, the Supreme Court determined that the judges went too far in attempting to remedy the discrimination; there were less extreme alternatives in each case. In *Jenkins*, the Court determined that the judge could order local officials to devise remedies, as per an opinion from the Court of Appeals. And in *Spallone*, the Court told the district judge that before sanctioning a legislature—an "extraordinary . . . imposition" (493 U.S. at 280)—the city should have been held accountable.

Again, the differences in the landmark and non-landmark news pegs show that the three newspapers have different metrics for determining newsworthiness; consequently, there is only a cascading effect or convergence on a minimum number of cases. Moreover, there does not seem to be any particular trend that aids in defining these metrics.

October Term 1996

As noted in chapter 3, the October Term 1996 saw a dip in overall coverage of the Court and its docket, and this dip occurs at the same time that we see the number of cases heard by the Court diminishing. Only 79 cases were heard with oral argument during this term, and 14% (11) of the cases were identified as landmark. The total number of stories for this term was 171, and a little over 50% (88) of these stories reported about a landmark decision. There is a major difference in focus compared to our three previous sample terms; the stories on this subset of cases only represented about a quarter (or less) of the total. As in previous terms, the largest percentage of the landmark cases centers on the First Amendment (31%), followed closely by the right to privacy (28%). Civil rights and criminal procedure, though, are not present among the landmarks. Instead, economic activity (22%) and federalism (10%) are the other large placeholders, although we would argue that this categorization is more or less consistent with the direction of the Rehnquist Court. Ten years into Chief Justice Rehnquist's tenure in the center chair, and the landmark cases, at least in this Term, seem to fall into areas that formed Rehnquist's legacy.

The First Amendment cases generated 33 total stories, but these were spread out over four separate cases. Garnering the most coverage was *Reno v. ACLU* (521 U.S. 844 [1997]), then *City of Boerne v. Flores* (521 U.S. 507 [1997]), with *Agostini v. Felton* (521 U.S. 203 [1997]) and *Turner Broadcasting System v. FCC* (520 U.S. 180 [1997]) bringing up the rear. Each case dealt with a different portion of the First Amendment. In *Reno*, the Court struck down two provisions of Congress's first attempt at quashing the distribution of obscene material to minors via the Internet. As is often the case with first tries, the Court determined that the law was too vague, particularly its definition of indecency, and therefore trampled on the rights of adults even if the intention was to protect children.

The Landmark Cases   **77**

Continuing its trend of chipping away at the wall separating church and state, the Court ruled in *Agostini* that the Establishment Clause is not automatically violated when a public school teacher is sent into a parochial school to instruct students. The new doctrine, developed here by Justice O'Connor, determined that the Establishment Clause is only violated if the state action or policy creates excessive conflict or entanglement between religion and government. The last case also dealt with the First Amendment and religion, and is classified as a free exercise case.

In *City of Boerne v. Flores*, the Court struck down parts of the *Religious Freedom and Restoration Act* of 1993 (RFRA) as exceeding congressional authority under the Equal Protection and Due Process Clauses. The Equal Protection Clause provides power for remedial or proscriptive legislation, and does not provide Congress the authority to determine how a state respects that amendment—just that it does so. Here Congress wanted to protect free exercise by preempting laws that "substantially burden[ed] a person's exercise of religion even if the burden results from a rule of general applicability, except as provided in subsection (b) of this section" (42 U.S.C. § 2000bb-1). In the subsection, the law required that any burden on religion must meet the requirements of strict scrutiny—the doctrine that the Court developed to protect fundamental rights. After the Court ruled in *Smith* during the 1989 Term and changed the test applied to free exercise claims when dealing with generally applicable laws, Congress reacted and passed RFRA, essentially ordering the federal courts to disregard *Smith*. The challenge here came when a Catholic church wished to renovate its building, but was denied because it was located in an historical district and was subject to strict rules for the alteration of historic structures. The church sued, essentially claiming a burden on its First Amendment rights, but using RFRA as its vehicle. Rather than bowing to this overt congressional pressure, the Court voided portions of the law. The Court used a comparison between the *Voting Rights Act* of 1965, where it allowed a significant infringement on state sovereignty because of the overwhelming evidence of discriminatory practices and the lack of success with less extreme measures. In *City of Boerne*, Justice Kennedy wrote, there is no history or rash of infringements on religious freedom and the historic preservation laws here only incidentally burden religion. "RFRA is so out of proportion to a supposed remedial or preventive object that it cannot be understood as responsive to, or designed to prevent, unconstitutional behavior."

Finally, in *Turner Broadcasting System*, the Court upheld the 1992 *Cable Television Consumer Protection and Competition Act* that required cable providers to carry local broadcast stations. The government's interest in program diversity and ensuring a competitive market were sufficient to overcome the claim of imposed speech upon the cable companies.

The two right to privacy cases are closely related and deal with the issues surrounding euthanasia, and more specifically physician-assisted suicide. Both

78 The Landmark Cases

Washington v. Glucksberg (521 U.S. 702 [1997]) and *Vacco v. Quill* (521 U.S. 793 [1997]) considered state laws banning the practice of physician-assisted suicide. Glucksberg argued for a fundamental right to die, including dying with a physician's aid, under the Due Process Clause. Quill argued a similar question using an equal protection approach and claimed that since New York allows the refusal of extraordinary measures or medical treatment that leads to death, a refusal which is "essentially the same thing as physician assisted suicide," preventing physician-assisted suicide treats similarly situated people differently. In both cases, the Court applied the rational basis test, acknowledging that the state laws were rationally related to the legitimate interest of supporting our legal traditions. According to the Court, the "penumbras and emanations" forming the right to privacy do not include the fundamental right to die.

There were two landmark cases in the economic activity pool. One case, *Clinton v. Jones* (520 U.S. 681 [1997]), generated 18 of the 21 stories about economic activity. We noted above that we feel this category name is a bit of a misnomer for this case because the subject matter of the case (liability and civil procedure) was not what earned it landmark status. Rather it was the players, specifically one player, which ensured that this case would make headlines, gain salience, and achieve notice as a landmark. As was the case with *United States v. Eichmann*, this is another instance where the Court finds itself embroiled in a political drama, and its role in the legal chapter of this drama is outsized due to politicians using the scandal and the legal battle for political gain.

Clinton v. Jones dealt with allegations of sexual harassment against President Clinton stemming from actions while he was still governor of Arkansas. Claiming that allowing the case to continue would affect his and his successors' ability to govern, President Clinton argued that the case should be deferred until after his term or terms as president ended.[7] The Court did not accept the president's arguments noting that there is no unqualified immunity for those occupying the oval office.

The other economic activity landmark case was less sensational—and how could it not be? *United States v. O'Hagan* (521 U.S. 642 [1997]) dealt with Securities and Exchange Commission rules and fraudulent trading, as well as money laundering and mail fraud. Justice Ginsburg, writing for the Court, reversed the Court of Appeals for the Eighth Circuit and allowed the use of the misappropriation theory of securities fraud.

The 10% of stories falling into the category of federalism, like the economic activity category, were derived from one important state's rights case: *Printz v. United States* (521 U.S. 898 [1997]). Here, the Court said in no uncertain terms that Congress cannot directly command state chief law enforcement officers to undertake a federal task, regardless of the temporary nature of the requirement. As we noted earlier, the Rehnquist Court is known for its support of state power vis-à-vis federal incursion, and the *Printz* case is a prime example of this doctrine.

News Pegs

In terms of news pegs, coverage of the decisions from the 1996 Term seems to be more equal across cases. There were few decisions that met the threshold for a news peg for any of the papers. During the 1975, 1985, and 1989 Terms, there were a total of 9, 11, and 10 unique news pegs, respectively. For the 1996 Term, however, there were only five decisions that generated enough coverage to meet our news peg criterion. The *New York Times* pegged two cases, and the *Los Angeles Times* pegged only one. The *Washington Post* had saturated coverage on a total of five cases. Additionally, the newspapers did not converge on any particular case. The *New York Times* and the *Post* pegged *Clinton v. Jones*—not terribly surprising. The *Post* and the *Los Angeles Times* significantly overreported on the *Glucksberg* case, with the *Post* also pegging *Vacco v. Quill*. Given the battles over federal power in both *City of Boerne* and *Printz*, it is again unsurprising that the *Post* had saturated coverage of these two cases. After all, the Court voided major federal legislation in both cases, and the *Post*, with its location in the nation's capital, would be more likely to focus on these two landmark cases.

Turning to a comparison of landmark cases with non-landmark cases, we find that civil rights stories rather than the First Amendment led the coverage for this term for the non-landmark category. Twenty-eight percent of the less momentous cases were related to civil rights. Cases touching upon the right to privacy were second here, as they were in the landmark subset (18%). Criminal procedure (13%) and First Amendment (11%) round out the substantive areas that receive at least 10% of the coverage of the non-landmark cases.

Only one non-landmark case rose to the threshold for a news peg. The *New York Times* significantly overreported the case of *Richardson & Walker v. McKnight* (521 U.S. 399 [1997]). This case seems an unlikely subject for a news peg. McKnight was a prisoner at the South Central Correction Center in Tennessee. At some point, he was transferred to another prison where prison guards Richardson and Walker restrained him. According to McKnight, they did so in violation of his Eighth Amendment rights; specifically, McKnight claimed the restraints were too tight. In its decision, the Court applied a recent precedent, *Wyatt v. Cole* (504 U.S. 158 [1992]), and determined that since the state of Tennessee had contracted with a private firm to run its prison facilities, *Wyatt*'s finding that private defendants are not immune from civil suits held. In other words, the state did not hire the prison guards. Therefore, they were not state employees and did not enjoy qualified immunity from a constitutional tort suit. It is not clear why the *New York Times* made this decision such a focus of its coverage. As the case comes from Tennessee, there is no regional connection to explain the *New York Times* saturation coverage. One story about this case came from the Court reporter, at this point Linda Greenhouse; staff reporters wrote the rest of the stories. Although none of the other papers we examine reported on the decision, CBS covered the case.

80 The Landmark Cases

Clearly, then, the *New York Times* was not completely out on a limb. CBS, as we have discussed elsewhere, only covered 14 cases that term.

October Term 2006

By the October Term 2006, the reduction in the Court's docket is now the norm. During this term, the Court heard a total of 75 merits cases—66 with oral argument. Seven landmark cases emerge from this total, accounting for 9% of the merits cases. Overall coverage of the landmark cases resembles the 1996 term with 48% (101) of all news stories (210) reflecting these seven landmark decisions. Dominating this coverage are news stories reporting on right to privacy cases (34%); more specifically all 34 stories reflect a major decision in the continuing abortion debate: *Gonzales v. Carhart* (550 U.S. 124 [2007]). *Gonzales*—with a 5–4 majority and the swing vote, Justice Kennedy, writing for the Court—determined that the federal *Partial Birth Abortion Ban Act* of 1995 was constitutional. By reading the statute narrowly so it applied only to one type of procedure—a procedure that Congress found was never a medical necessity and therefore did not need a health exception for the mother—the Court saved the federal ban from the same fate a Nebraska law suffered in *Stenberg v. Carhart* (530 U.S. 914 [2000]). The *New York Times* was responsible for almost half of the stories on the federal case (47%) with only CBS accounting for less than 10% of the stories (three).

Civil rights cases make up 25% of the news stories (25) and are almost evenly split between a major employment discrimination/equal pay case (13) and a groundbreaking affirmative action case (12). Lilly Ledbetter had sued Goodyear for salary discrimination under Title VII of the 1964 *Civil Rights Act*. She was paid less than similarly situated men for the same work. She did not file formal charges until 1998, though she began work for Goodyear in 1979. Since Goodyear did not make salaries public, Ledbetter did not know until right before she retired that she was making less than her male colleagues. Although she won in the lower courts, the Supreme Court reversed. Reading Title VII narrowly, the Court determined that the statute of limitations for Ledbetter's claim had expired. Even though she was unaware of the discrepancy, the legal clock began to tick upon receipt of her first discriminatory check. In other words, the first incidence of pay discrimination starts the 180-day clock (*Ledbetter v. Goodyear Tire & Rubber Co.* 550 U.S. 618 [2007]). In one of the first legislative acts of his presidency, Barack Obama signed the *Lilly Ledbetter Fair Pay Act* of 2009. The legislation clarifies that the statute of limitations resets with each discriminatory paycheck.

In a bitter defeat for supporters of affirmative action, Chief Justice Roberts refused to extend the logic and reasoning of *Grutter v. Bollinger* (539 U.S. 306 [2003]) in *Parents Involved in Community Schools v. Seattle School District No. 1* (551 U.S. 701 [2007]). Ruling that the decisions regarding affirmative action and higher education do not carry to the public schools, the Court voided Seattle's racial tiebreaker policy since it, unlike the policy at the University of

The Landmark Cases **81**

Michigan School of Law at issue in *Grutter*, did not examine the individual students, used a limited definition of diversity, and was more related to demographic goals than the educational benefits of diversity. Moreover, Roberts held, the plan was not narrowly tailored to serve a compelling governmental interest; therefore it violated the equal protection rights of students denied admission to their school of choice solely due to their race. In dissent Justice Stevens put his view starkly:

> The Court has changed significantly since it decided *School Comm. of Boston* in 1968. It was then more faithful to *Brown* and more respectful of our precedent than it is today. It is my firm conviction that no Member of the Court that I joined in 1975 would have agreed with today's decision. (551 U.S. at 803)

One case coming under the rubric of judicial power was mentioned in some 20 stories (20%), and this case resulted from a long-standing argument between environmental activists and the Bush administration. In this case it was Massachusetts, rather than a public interest group, leading the charge. Throughout the Bush administration, the federal Environmental Protection Agency (EPA) asserted that it did not have the authority to regulate carbon emissions under the *Clean Air Act* of 1970 (as amended in 1990). Massachusetts brought suit, and when it reached the Court, the question at hand was whether the EPA had the authority to regulate these emissions. The Court did not direct the EPA to regulate the emissions, but it did note that the agency does indeed have the power under the *Clean Air Act* and ordered the EPA to consider "whether greenhouse gas emissions contribute to climate change." In other words, under the *Clean Air Act* the EPA does not have to regulate, but the decision to impose or not to impose regulation must be answered by scientific empirical analysis rather than policy concerns.

Two First Amendment cases generated 18 stories (18%): *Morse v. Frederick* (551 U.S. 393 [2007]) and *FEC v. Wisconsin Right to Life* (551 U.S. 449 [2007]). *Morse* is characterized as a protest demonstration case. As the Olympic torch went through Juneau, Alaska, the local high school students were permitted to leave class and attend the event. Joseph Frederick, a senior, unveiled a large sign as the torch and television cameras passed by; the sign read, "BONG HITS 4 JESUS." The principal, Deborah Morse, interpreted the sign as supporting the taking of illegal drugs. Given the school's zero tolerance policy, Morse confiscated the banner and suspended Frederick for lack of compliance with a request to lower the banner. After losing an appeal within the school system, Frederick sued the principal and the school board for violation of his free speech rights. Speaking for the Court, Chief Justice Roberts noted that the Court considered this a school speech case. Under *Tinker v. Des Moines* (393 U.S. 503 [1969]), therefore, and given the principal's reasonable interpretation that the sign was supporting illegal drug use, the suppression of Frederick's speech was constitutional. Morse's actions serve a

82 The Landmark Cases

compelling government interest, deterring drug abuse among students, and "allow schools to restrict student expression that they reasonably regard as promoting illegal drug use" (551 U.S. at 407).

In a run up to the 2010 blockbuster case of *Citizens United* (558 U.S. 310 [2010]), the Court decided in *FEC v. Wisconsin Right to Life* that the *Bipartisan Campaign Reform Act*'s ban on corporate-funded issue ads in the days immediately preceding an election was unconstitutional. Ruling that these ads are not political advocacy but rather issue advocacy, the Court determined that an ad is political advocacy only if the ad "is susceptible of no reasonable interpretation other than as an appeal to vote for or against a specific candidate" (551 U.S. at 465). The state's interests in preventing corruption or curtailing the role of corporate monies in elections was not compelling enough to allow the violation of the First Amendment rights of the corporations.

Economic activity, specifically antitrust action, was the only category that did not encompass at least 10% of the stories. *Leegin Creative Leather Products v. PSKS* (551 U.S. 877 [2007]) is a *Sherman Antitrust Act* case where the Court determined that mandatory minimum prices do not automatically violate the Act. A landmark case for business and antitrust law, *Leegin* was only covered in four stories: two in the *New York Times* and two in the *Los Angeles Times*.

News Pegs

All three newspapers provided significant coverage to *Massachusetts v. EPA* (549 U.S. 497 [2007]) and, as expected, *Gonzales v. Carhart*, both cases meeting our criterion for a news peg. Overall, however, the trend we observed for the 1996 Term continued in this term. The newspapers were pegging fewer cases. It is unclear whether the decline in the overall number of saturated cases is a result of the Court's shrinking docket, reductions in column inches, more equivalent coverage across all cases covered, or some other factor we have not yet contemplated, although the declining attention of the newspapers to the Court observed by Lyle Denniston seems a likely culprit (see Strickler 2014, 155). Regardless, *Gonzales v. Carhart* and *Massachusetts v. EPA* were the only two cases the *New York Times* pegged. Both the *Los Angeles Times* and *Washington Post* provided saturated coverage for three cases. In addition to the two cases mentioned earlier, the *Los Angeles Times* dedicated appreciable coverage to *Parents Involved in Community Schools v. Seattle* (551 U.S. 701 [2007]). Given this paper's tendency to overreport on stories that are generated close to home and the salience of the affirmative action issue, this finding is not at all unexpected. The *Post*'s third news peg was not a landmark case. In *Phillip Morris USA v. Williams* (549 U.S. 346 [2007]), "[t]he question we address today concerns a large state-court punitive damages award. We are asked whether the Constitution's Due Process Clause permits a jury to base that award in part upon its desire to *punish* the defendant for harming persons who are not

The Landmark Cases **83**

before the court (e.g., victims whom the parties do not represent)" (551 U.S. at 349). Writing for the Court, Justice Breyer found that when a jury uses its power to award such damages for harms outside of the instant case, it is a violation of due process and the Takings Clause.

In the subset of non-landmark cases, we see a new substantive area take the lead. Economic activity cases total 35% of all the coverage here (119 cases). Criminal procedure cases, as seems to be the norm, are also given heavy coverage (29%). Judicial power cases and First Amendment cases round out the top four in this subset (13% and 11%). And as reported above, only one case from this subset rose to the level of a news peg.

Conclusion

The press, it seems, followed a pattern of saturated coverage similar to what we described in chapter 3 within the subset of cases deemed "landmark." We are not suggesting that these cases are not newsworthy; however, the effect of such saturation is distinct. These issue areas and cases define the Court in the public's mind and influence specific and diffuse or overall support for the Court as an institution. As Iyengar, Peters, and Kinder (1982) have shown, the more heavily reported an issue, the higher it reaches on the public's agenda. And if an individual does not have a great deal of foreknowledge about an issue or case, the media may be able to go beyond educating and agenda setting to persuasion. While we doubt that the limited coverage of the Court can sway many, even in those limited cases that serve as news pegs, simply setting the agenda—shaping the public's perception of the Court and its work—can be detrimental to the overall legitimacy of the institution. Continued attention to salient issue areas rather than to critical cases skews the image of the Court. Combine these hot potato issues with increases in the reporting on the "cult of personality" and we have a worrying trend.

Notes

1 As noted in Chapter 3, a "news peg" is simply an indicator of over-coverage of a case or an issue. (For a more detailed discussion see, for example, Clawson et al. 2003).
2 The statistical analyses reported in this paragraph exclude 2009, inasmuch as *Congressional Quarterly* included only two landmark cases from that very recent term.
3 As noted earlier, the list for the October Term 2009 is incomplete. During that term, there were cases dealing with the right to privacy—such as *City of Ontario v. Quon*, No. 08-1332 (which determined the scope of privacy rights for text messages on a government electronic device) and *McDonald v. Chicago*, No. 08-1521 (where the Court incorporated the Second Amendment)—that are likely to make a list of landmark cases from that term.
4 A distinct decision has its own docket number and *United States Reports* number.
5 This language comes from the interim rules in 47 Fed. Reg. 26027 (1982); similar language was placed in the Final Rules in February 1984.

84 The Landmark Cases

6 See Heather Mason Kiefer, "Support Cooling for Flag-Burning Amendment," Gallup, July 26, 2005, www.gallup.com/poll/17491/support-cooling-flagburning-amendment.aspx (last accessed March 10, 2014).
7 In some senses, the president and his lawyers were correct. The eventual continuation of this case leads to testimony by Monica Lewinsky and Lewinsky's taped conversations with Linda Tripp. These, once delivered to Special Prosecutor Kenneth Starr, led to Clinton's impeachment in 1998.

References

Clawson, Rosalee A., Harry C. N. Strine IV, and Eric N. Waltenburg. 2003. "Framing Supreme Court Decisions: The Mainstream Versus the Black Press." *Journal of Black Studies* 33 (6):784–800.

Cohen, Jacob. 1992. "A Power Primer." *Psychological Bulletin* 112 (1):155–59.

Epstein, Lee, and Jeffrey A. Segal. 2000. "Measuring Issue Salience." *American Journal of Political Science* 44 (1):66–83.

Iyengar, Shanto, Mark D. Peters, and Donald R. Kinder. 1982. "Experimental Demonstrations of the 'Not-So-Minimal' Consequences of Television News Programs." *American Political Science Review* 74 (4):848–58.

Solberg, Rorie L., and Eric N. Waltenburg. 2014. "Constructing Harry Blackmun." In *Covering the United States Supreme Court in the Digital Age*, pp. 109–125. ed. R. Davis. New York: Oxford University Press.

Strickler, Richard James. 2014. "The Supreme Court and New Media Technologies." In *Covering the United States Supreme Court in the Digital Age*, pp. 61–88. ed. R. Davis. New York: Cambridge University Press.

Vining, Jr., Richard L., and Phil Marcin. 2014. "Explaining Intermedia Coverage of Supreme Court Decisions." In *Covering the United States Supreme Court in the Digital Age*, pp. 89–108. ed. R. Davis. New York: Cambridge University Press.

5

THE PERSONAL MYTH

In chapters 3 and 4, we showed the media presents a distorted image of the Court's outputs, overreporting certain cases and issues and (more central to our thesis) increasingly including in its stories on Court decisions elements essential to what we have identified as the "cult of personality." This greater emphasis on the personal and political aspects surrounding a decision has not replaced the media's use of symbols associated with the "cult of the robe"—reporting on the legal or institutional justifications for a decision as well as references to its legal implications—but it does present the public with a far more variegated picture of the Court. Is a similar media effect present with respect to coverage of individual justices? There are good reasons to expect this to be the case. First, just as certain types of decisions (because of the issue involved or the legal, political, or social implications of the outcome) are more apt to attract media attention, so too are certain moments in the career life cycle of a justice. Nominations, confirmations, and retirements are obvious examples. They are highly unique events that are focused on the individual. Consequently, these are the instances when the media's spotlight should be most intense. Second, outside of these very personal career events, the newsworthiness of a justice largely is tied to his or her role in the Court's outputs. And since we uncovered a growing frequency of media coverage of politics in its stories on Court decisions, there is a strong likelihood that mentions of the individual justice will shade more and more toward the "cult of personality" over time as well. After all, the individual justice is the object to which the personal and the politics of the Court can be tied.

In this chapter we explore the media's coverage of the individual justice. Specifically, we analyze the *New York Times*'s coverage of Justices Harry Blackmun and John Paul Stevens across the entirety of their career life cycles. Our chapter is

86 The Personal Myth

organized as follows. We begin with a description of our data and research design. We then turn to an examination of the *Times*'s mentions of either justice. We find that its coverage of Justices Blackmun and Stevens is uneven. Both justices are more newsworthy at the ends of their careers on the Bench. (Blackmun is also especially newsworthy at the time of his nomination and in relation to the Court's abortion decisions.) Otherwise the justices are mentioned largely in relation to the Court's work. We also find an increasing frequency of *Times* stories mentioning either justice to include elements of the "cult of personality," but these references do not occur in isolation from stories reporting on the Court's decisions. We conclude by reviewing our findings and pointing out the dissonance created by the simultaneous presence of both myths.

Data and Research Design

To explore the media's coverage of an individual Supreme Court justice, we mined the Proquest Historical Newspapers archive for *New York Times* articles mentioning either Justice Harry Blackmun or John Paul Stevens from one year prior to his appointment to the Court through the year following his retirement from the High Bench. Our focus on the *Times*'s coverage of these particular Supreme Court justices' life cycles offers us an excellent sample of the incidence and nature of the media's treatment of individual justices. First, as the national paper of record, the *New York Times* is a highly credible and representative source (Althaus, Edy, and Phalen 2001). Moreover, it provides more complete coverage of the Court than almost any other newspaper, and certainly more than any electronic medium (see chapter 3; Slotnick and Segal 1998; Spill and Oxley 2003). Second, Blackmun and Stevens were appointed to and announced their retirements from the High Bench in the midst of a Court term. Thus, we are able to compare the media's coverage of these more personal, made-for-media moments in a justice's career to the attention the media gives to the everyday business and workings of the Court—i.e., the Court's decisions and the opinions and orders of the justices—across a series of terms.

To ensure we captured every relevant article, we cast our net broadly and conducted separate searches for each justice. For Blackmun, we searched the Proquest archives from April 14, 1969, through August 3, 1995; for Stevens, from November 28, 1974, through June 29, 2011.[1] This search strategy identified 3,314 articles: 1,611 articles mentioning Blackmun and 1,703 articles mentioning Stevens. Each article was then coded for *how* it mentioned either justice—for example, whether he voted with the majority or dissented, whether he wrote an opinion, if some personal information about the justice was conveyed, or if a reference was made to the justice's ideological position or legal philosophy.[2] Up to three mentions per article were coded. This resulted in a data set of 4,013 total mentions of the justices, 1,945 mentions of Blackmun (about 1.2 mentions per article or

70 mentions per year) and 2,068 mentions of Stevens (again, about 1.2 mentions per article, or 56 mentions per year); the mean annual rates of mentions for the justices are significantly different ($|t|$ = 2.42, p < 0.02).[3] That Blackmun's mean number of mentions per year is significantly greater than Stevens's is consistent with Davis's finding that Blackmun received the greatest percentage of mentions in the *Times* for all the justices between 1986 and 2007 (2011, 161; Table 6.4). Finally, in the case of both justices, the vast majority of the stories made only one mention. Accordingly, for Justice Blackmun, only 19.6% of the stories contained a second mention, and just a tick over 1% of the stories had three mentions. Mentions of Justice Stevens follow a similar pattern. Nearly 19% of the articles contain a second mention; only 3.6% include a third reference to the justice. Given the rare occurrence of third mentions, the analysis and discussion that follows concentrates on the first and second mentions.

Analysis

We begin by examining separately the distribution of the *Times*'s first and second mentions of each justice. When it comes to first mentions, it is clear that the justices' voting behavior and opinion authorship attract the greatest amount of newsprint. In Justice Blackmun's case (see Figure 5.1a), more than one-third of the first mentions concern his alignment with a decision's majority, either as a voting member (24%) or as the author of the majority opinion itself (11%). Likewise, Blackmun's dissenting behavior attains first mention status with some frequency. His votes in the minority are mentioned first over 12% of the time, and his authorship of a dissenting opinion is mentioned first about 7% of the time. Finally, it is noteworthy that personal information about Justice Blackmun is mentioned first in over 8% of the stories making reference to him in our data set. Indeed, it is the fourth most frequently occurring first mention category. By way of contrast, personal information on Justice Stevens is mentioned first in only 4.5% of the stories referring to him (see Figure 5.1b). A difference in proportions test indicates that the percentage of first mentions reporting personal information in articles on Blackmun is significantly greater than is the percentage of personal information mentioned first for Justice Stevens (z = 4.37, p < 0.00).

What might account for the relatively high proportion of articles with personal information mentioned first for Justice Blackmun? Davis's discussion of the factors associated with the disproportionate amount of *New York Times* coverage mentioning Blackmun suggests three explanations: Blackmun's greater willingness to "go public" and interact with the media by giving speeches and granting interviews; his close association with *Roe v. Wade* (410 U.S. 113 [1973]) and the issue of abortion more generally; and his relationship with Linda Greenhouse (Davis 2011, 161–68).

88 The Personal Myth

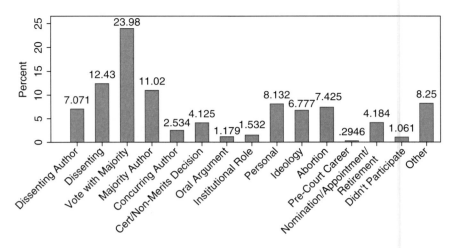

FIGURE 5.1A Distribution of First Mentions: Justice Harry Blackmun

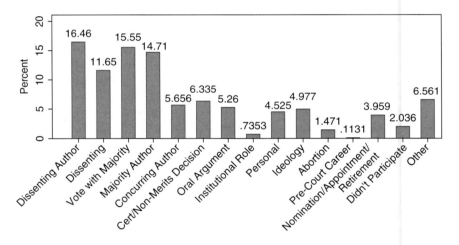

FIGURE 5.1B Distribution of First Mentions: Justice John Paul Stevens

First, although on the current Court it is not unusual for justices to directly engage with the media (see Davis 2011), Blackmun was something of a trendsetter in this regard. Indeed, as *Times* correspondent Stuart Taylor noted in 1983, Blackmun, more than his brethren, was willing to engage the media and, in turn, "most dramatically broke the ice of inaccessibility" that generally grips the Court and its members.[4] Consequently, Blackmun may have simply provided the *Times*'s reporters with more personal information to report. And these reporters, hungry to attach a human element to the story and/or seeking out personal or attitudinal motivations for his decisional behavior (see chapter 1 for a discussion of media practices and the new style of journalism), used it.

Second, as we discuss in greater detail below, Blackmun's identification with *Roe* and the politics of abortion resulted in greater press coverage mentioning him. Now, this coverage did not concentrate only on the judicial actions surrounding *Roe* and the line of decisions that resulted from conservative litigation efforts to overturn the precedent. There were a fair number of stories mentioning Blackmun that reported on the dramatic political events attendant to the polarizing issue, and it is in these stories that personal information on Blackmun is mentioned. For example, there is the 1985 story reporting on a letter sent by the Army of God threatening the justice with death and the concomitant increase in security for the justices.[5]

Finally, Davis points out Blackmun developed a personal friendship with Linda Greenhouse, the Court reporter for the *Times* during most of his tenure; she eventually became his biographer (2011, 166).[6] Davis argues that the significant coverage the *Times* devoted to Blackmun was the result of what might be perceived as a "Greenhouse effect." He notes that together with their friendship, Greenhouse was highly supportive of Blackmun's judicial stance on a woman's reproductive rights. Moreover, according to Davis, the *Times*'s attention to Blackmun was probably Greenhouse's editorial decision rather than the decisions of wire service editors. These forces combined to make "Blackmun a star of *New York Times* Supreme Court coverage" (2011, 166, 168).

Along with frequency, was there a similar "Greenhouse effect" at work with respect to the *nature* of the mentions of Justice Blackmun in the *Times*? After all, it seems quite possible that Greenhouse was privy to a deep reservoir of personal information on the justice, and this information found its way into her stories for the *Times* that mention him. Our data suggest, however, that this is not the case. Indeed, articles written by Linda Greenhouse have a significantly lower proportion of first mentions containing personal information on Justice Blackmun than articles under any other byline ($z = 4.39$, $p < 0.00$).[7] Thus, it seems Blackmun's attentiveness to the media and his close association with *Roe v. Wade*—arguably the most politically charged decision since *Brown v. Board of Education* (347 U.S. 483 [1954])—resulted in his significant proportion of personal first mentions.

Just as an aspect of Justice Blackmun's personality and behavior is reflected in the distribution of the *Times*'s mentions of him, so too is a defining attribute of Justice Stevens. Stevens was well known for his independent and maverick status on the Court. Indeed, in a speech at a conference of federal judges and lawyers in 1988, Justice Blackmun referred to his colleague in just that way: "Stevens, I think, is still kind of a maverick on the Court. He is imaginative. He writes a lot, writes well, and he's always interested in the theory of the case."[8] Stevens's independence often materialized in a tendency both to dissent and to write separate opinions. In fact, during his tenure on the Bench, Stevens wrote a special opinion in 27% of

90 The Personal Myth

the decisions in which he participated—a rate of authorship greater than that of any justice with whom he served and significantly different from the mean ($|t|$ = 8.93, p < 0.00). His maverick or imaginative streak, however, probably limited his influence on the Court and on the law. Bill Barnhart and Gene Schlickman, Stevens's biographers, for example, quote Victor Blasi on this point:

> Stevens has tended to develop highly original, sometimes idiosyncratic theories that fail to win the endorsement of his brethren. He is a formidable but unconventional legal thinker. . . . [T]he effect of his independence of mind often has been to fragment potential majorities and leave the state of the law indeterminate. (Blasi 1983, 252; qtd. in Barnhart and Schlickman 2010, 229)

Whether Stevens left as deep a footprint on the law as he might have, given his more than three decades as a justice, one thing is certain: Stevens's propensity to write special opinions provided the media with substantial grist about which to report. Accordingly, Stevens's special opinions attain first mention status an appreciable amount of the time. The modal category of the *Times*'s first mentions of Stevens is his authorship of dissenting opinions, and his authorship of concurring opinions are mentioned first nearly 6% of the time (5.7%). Compare this to the 2.5% of first mentions dedicated to Blackmun's concurring opinions. To be sure, Stevens's presence in the majority is reported (15.6%), but when it is compared to the relative frequency of first mentions of Blackmun's majority votes (24%), Stevens's independence becomes especially apparent (see Figure 5.1b).

When we turn to the distributions of second mentions, we observe some interesting changes. Where voting in the majority coalition is the clear first-mention, modal category for Justice Blackmun, it is eclipsed by mentions of his majority opinion authorship in the second mention distribution. Voting, whether in the majority or minority, does remain a regularly mentioned category, with mentions of Blackmun's dissents and votes with the majority tied for the third most frequent appearance. Mentions of personal information about Harry Blackmun and references to his ideology acquire an especially notable presence in this distribution. Personal information, although retaining its fourth-place status, climbs to 10.5% of the second mentions. Meanwhile, mentions of ideology soar, accounting for nearly 16% of the second mentions and becoming the second largest category (see Figure 5.1c).

The increase in the relative frequency of second mentions concerning ideology and personal information is even more striking for the *Times*'s coverage of Justice Stevens. Where neither category tops 5% of first mentions, they become the two most frequent types of second mentions, accounting for nearly 20% and 13% of second mentions, respectively. As was the case with Justice Blackmun, Stevens's decisional behavior is not ignored in the second mentions. Collectively,

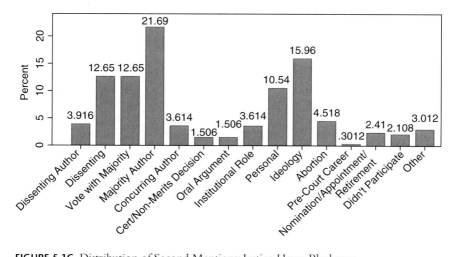

FIGURE 5.1C Distribution of Second Mentions: Justice Harry Blackmun

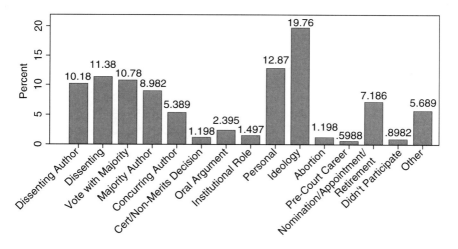

FIGURE 5.1D Distribution of Second Mentions: Justice John Paul Stevens

mentions of Stevens's votes and opinion authorship (i.e., five distinct categories) constitute nearly half of his second-mentions distribution (see Figure 5.1d).

We also observe that there is something of a seasonal component to the incidence and rate of these different categories of mentions. It is perhaps to state the obvious that the *Times* mentions the justices with greater frequency while the Court is in session. After all, since the Court is in session about three times longer than it is out of session, there are simply many more opportunities in which to mention the justices during a session. It is much more interesting, however, to note (first) that the *rate* at which the *Times* mentions the justices is not significantly different depending on whether the Court is in or out of session, and (second) mentions of ideology and personal information (i.e., the "cult of personality") loom large in the out-of-session coverage, accounting for over 40% of the total mentions ($z = 9.59; p < 0.00$). These two categories only account for about 15% of the mentions of the justices while the Court is in session.

It appears, then, that when mentioning individual justices, the *Times* couches those mentions in the context of the Court's business—the justices' decisions, their presence in voting blocs, and their authorship of opinions—*when there is business of the Court to report*. Yet, even when reporting on the Court's business, the *Times*'s stories include a nontrivial share of subsequent references (i.e., second mentions) that focus on judicial characteristics we have identified as aspects of the "cult of personality"—that is, references to some personal information about the justice, a nomination or confirmation, and ideological or attitudinal preferences. Indeed, nearly 11% of the articles we examine that contain a "cult of the robe" first mention have a "cult of personality" second mention. A 1971 article by Fred Graham is an excellent example. The first mention of Justice Blackmun concerns his presence in a narrow 5–4 majority that limited *Miranda* protections. Graham's second mention of Blackmun identifies him as part of an emerging conservative majority that was rounding into form as a result of the series of Nixon appointments. "The ruling today presented the strongest indication to date that President Nixon's appointment of Justice Blackmun has created the conservative majority on criminal law issues that Mr. Nixon has set as his goal."[9] And when there is little or no Supreme Court business or activity to report, mentions of the "cult of personality" soar. Finally, it bears noting that both the likelihood of a second mention of the justices appearing in a *Times* article and a mention dealing with an aspect of the "cult of personality" significantly increase at later dates in our data set—an observation displayed in Figures 5.2 and 5.3. Although only circumstantial, these

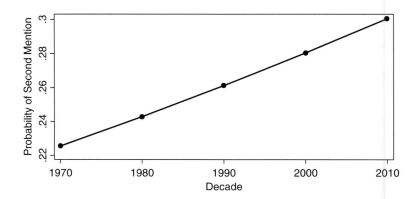

FIGURE 5.2 Increase in Probability of Second Mention

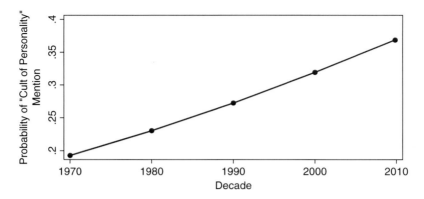

FIGURE 5.3 Increase in Probability of "Cult of Personality" Mention

data suggest that the *Times*'s coverage is more likely to focus on a justice's personal and political character over time. Adding to our confidence is that Davis finds a similar trend. "Basically what the two media—the *New York Times* and *NBC Nightly News*—discussed about the Court changed from an emphasis on cases to an emphasis on individuals" (2011, 159; see also table 6.2, p. 158).

The Patterns of Mentions

Given that the Court's business, and the justice's behavior with respect to it, tends to orient the *Times*'s coverage of individual justices, we would expect the incidence of total mentions of Justices Blackmun and Stevens to generally rise and fall in tandem over our time series. After all, as we have noted the tenures of Blackmun and Stevens substantially overlapped, and consequently they were mutually active on a vast amount of the Court's business in our data set. Thus, when Justice Blackmun participated in a case, so too did Justice Stevens, and the *Times* would mention both of these actions. Yet, the *Times*'s total mentions of the two justices are not at all collinear. Indeed, the correlation coefficient of total mentions across their common terms is both negative and vanishingly small (−.07).

To be sure, there is one clear temporal pattern present in both series (see Figure 5.4). Namely, the total mentions for each justice spikes in his final term and then falls precipitously with his departure from the Bench. But it is perhaps more interesting to note the differences in the time series. First, Blackmun's series exhibits a relatively large number of mentions at both its start and its end, indicating that Blackmun was perceived as especially newsworthy at both points in his career life cycle. Stevens's series, on the other hand, does not have a similar bookend pattern to its mentions. That Blackmun received more attention at the beginning of his association with the Supreme Court makes some sense, considering the extended confirmation battle swirling around the seat he eventually filled.

94 The Personal Myth

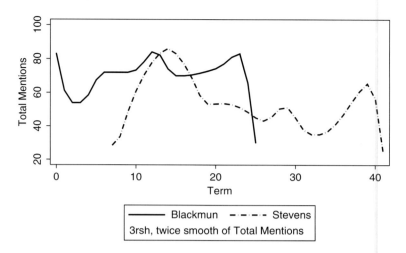

FIGURE 5.4 Total Mentions over Time: Justices Blackmun and Stevens

He was President Nixon's third choice, following the confirmation implosions of Haynsworth and Carswell. Gerald Ford's nomination of John Paul Stevens, on the other hand, faced no such controversy nor attracted much attention. Indeed, given Ford's weak political position—unelected himself; as a Republican, indirectly tainted by the Watergate scandal; and facing a filibuster-proof Democratic majority—he apparently chose Stevens in no small part because partisan or ideological forces would not be perceived as affecting his nomination and eventual appointment. This, in turn, "kept Stevens in the background as he was being measured for black robes" (Barnhart and Schlickman 2010, 183).

Mentions and Abortion. Second, although early on the series generally mirror one another, there is a point at which they diverge. This occurs at about Term 15 (1984/85), and it seems to be a consequence of the emergence of the issue of abortion on the national political scene.

In the 1980s Ronald Reagan and the Republican party brought the abolition of *Roe v. Wade* into the national political arena and then rode it to significant electoral success. The Republicans occupied the White House throughout the decade and held a majority in the Senate from the 97th through the 99th Congresses (1981–1987). Politically energized, pro-life groups began to mount a litigation campaign to overturn *Roe*, a campaign endorsed by the GOP. By 1983 this campaign began to bear some fruit, as the Court heard the first major effort to strike down *Roe*. That effort was rebuffed in *City of Akron v. Akron Center for Reproductive Health* (462 U.S. 416 [1983]), but with Reagan's reelection in 1984, the assault on *Roe* was by no means over.

Throughout the 1980s, *Roe*'s vulnerability would only grow. Already in *City of Akron*, the original 7–2 *Roe* majority had dropped by one, as Sandra Day O'Connor, Reagan's first Supreme Court appointee, voted to uphold a law imposing regulatory limits on abortion. Then, at the end of its 1985 Term, the Court revisited the issue in *Thornburgh v. American College of Obstetricians and Gynecologists* (476 U.S. 747 [1986]; see chapter 4 for a more detailed discussion). Once again, the Court voted to preserve *Roe*, but this time the *Roe* majority was reduced to a minimum winning coalition, as Warren Burger moved into opposition. Continued Republican control of the Presidency, coupled with the superannuated status of the slim pro-*Roe* majority,[10] placed the right to an abortion on a very thin branch, and time appeared to be sawing away. All of this brought the attention of the *New York Times* to the fate of abortion before the Court. Moreover, that attention focused on Harry Blackmun.

As we have noted elsewhere (Solberg and Waltenburg 2014), few Supreme Court justices are as closely identified with a single case as Harry Blackmun is with *Roe v. Wade*. It became his legacy, a status he recognized. "I'll carry Roe against Wade to my grave, even though I think I've contributed a little bit in other areas of law," Blackmun once remarked while speaking at the Aspen Center.[11] Consequently, it was only natural for the *Times* to mention Blackmun in its coverage of the politics of the abortion issue writ large (i.e., protests over abortion, electoral politics, confirmation battles). Furthermore, it was in this coverage that Blackmun's legacy as the "author of *Roe*" was constructed, *not* news stories on litigation challenging *Roe* itself (Solberg and Waltenburg 2014). Thus, although the *Times* reported on the judicial behavior of both Justices Blackmun and Stevens in cases raising the issue of abortion, Blackmun, as the "author of Roe," gained additional mentions in those stories that went beyond simply reporting on the decisions themselves. Accordingly, stories referring to the votes, opinions, or questions in oral argument comprise the modal category of abortion mentions for both justices. In the case of Blackmun, they make up nearly 40% of the abortion-related mentions. For Justice Stevens, on the other hand, this category accounts for two-thirds of the abortion-related mentions. Meanwhile, stories that report on the *politics* of abortion or stories expressing some philosophical or political position regarding abortion compose about 25% of Blackmun's distribution; they nearly fail to register in the case of Justice Stevens—rising to a mere 10%. One result of these very different distributions: between Terms 13 (1982/83, when *City of Akron* was decided) and 22 (1992/93, the term in which *Planned Parenthood v. Casey* (505 U.S. 833 [1992] was handed down), Blackmun averaged nearly 3.2 times as many mentions related to abortion as Stevens. This difference between the justices' means just misses conventional levels of statistical significance (t = 2.04; p < .06).

The Tone or Nature of Mentions

This detailed analysis of the difference between the justices in the mentions related to abortion raises the question: Was the general nature of the *Times*'s coverage of each justice comparable? One way to explore this is to examine the mentions of

96 The Personal Myth

the justices concerning their work on the Court and those mentions that do not deal with Court-related work.[12]

Figure 5.5 displays the patterns of mentions of Court work and non-Court work for both justices over time. Several features are noteworthy. First, in the case of each justice, there is a steady increase in the frequency of mentions related to their work on the Court over their initial terms. Second, both justices experience an appreciable uptick in the incidence of their Court work mentions near the end of their tenure. This is especially interesting in light of the fact that mentions regarding retirement are not included; they fall into the category of non-Court work mentions. To be sure, both justices' non-Court work series exhibit an increase at the conclusion of the justices' tenures as well, no doubt a consequence of their retirement announcements and concomitant stories. However, that stories oriented specifically by the justices' work on the Court increase in frequency at the end of both series suggests that justices become more newsworthy as they emerge as the senior justice or in general as they approach the end of their career life cycles. Third, with the exception of the tremendous amount of mentions at the start of Blackmun's series (as we noted above, most likely a consequence of the political tempest surrounding the vacancy he was picked to fill), the non-Court work mentions for both justices are relatively meager, bouncing along the bottom of the figure, well below the frequency of mentions given to their work on the Court. Fourth, the frequency of Blackmun's non-Court work mentions is consistently greater than the non-Court work mentions of Stevens—perhaps a function of Blackmun's greater willingness to interact with the media and/or his association with *Roe* (see the discussion above). It is also interesting to

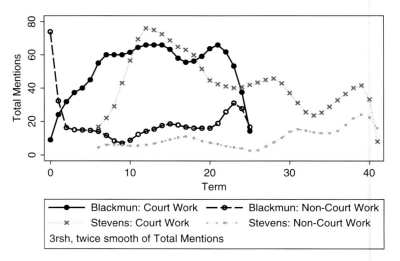

FIGURE 5.5 Total Mentions of Court Work and Non-Court Work: Justices Blackmun and Stevens

note that when Blackmun left the Court, the non-Court work mentions of Stevens climbed to their greatest levels, attaining frequencies comparable to those that Blackmun had experienced. This is perhaps a result of the recognition that with Blackmun's departure, Stevens became the most senior justice anchoring the Court's liberal bloc.

Media Storms

Finally, are there periods of heightened media attention paid to either justice, and if so, what types of events bring about this greater attention? Now, to a degree we have already presented some data bearing upon these questions. After all, the trends displayed in Figures 5.4 and 5.5 illustrate that Blackmun captured the attention of the *New York Times* during his confirmation and with respect to the increasing politicization of the abortion issue in the 1980s and early 1990s, and both justices were mentioned with relatively greater frequency at the end of their tenures. Here, however, we seek to bring a bit more analytical rigor to our query by investigating the occurrence of "media storms" in the *New York Times*'s mentions of Justices Blackmun and Stevens—that is, *appreciable surges or increases in the amount of attention the* Times *paid to a justice for some defined period of time*.[13] We operationalize a media storm as those instances where the mean frequency for any rolling seven-day period of *Times* mentions of either justice is more than two standard deviations greater than the mean frequency for that justice's full series.[14] This resulted in the identification of 110 storm days for Justice Blackmun and 141 storm days for Justice Stevens.

The distributions of the focus of the stories that produce storm level mentions of either justice are displayed in Figure 5.6. Nominations, confirmations, and retirements have a notable presence. These are very rare events, and they are concentrated on the individual. Thus, it is not surprising that mentions of either justice would spike during these occasions. But stories that cover Court decisions are far and away the modal category—further evidence that the Court's outputs orient the *Times*'s attention to these justices. No decision in a particular issue area, however, triggers a storm. Decisions running the gamut from state banking regulation and patent rights to deportation of an accused Nazi war criminal and doctor-assisted suicide are reported during days identified as media storms.[15]

Rather than certain types of issues acting as catalysts for a media storm, it appears to be the point during the Court's term that the decisions are announced that results in the surge of concomitant attention paid to Justices Blackmun and Stevens. Simply put, the typical crush of decisions at the end of the Court's term produces the heightened frequency of mentions. Indeed, nearly 71% of the days identified as media storms for Justice Blackmun occur during the final month of the Court's term, and the end-of-term frequency of storm days is even greater for Justice Stevens—nearly 88%. The gamma measure of association between the

98 The Personal Myth

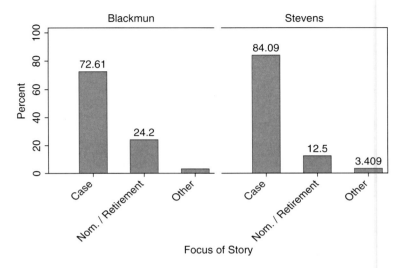

FIGURE 5.6 Focus of Media Storm Stories

end of the term and the occurrence of a media storm day is extremely strong and highly significant for both justices. For Blackmun, gamma is .91 (p < .00); for Stevens gamma is .97 (p < .00).

That there is a surge in attention given to the Court's outputs, and therefore an increase in the frequency of mentions of the justices, simultaneous with the Court simply announcing more decisions is of little surprise or analytical value. What is of far more interest to our thesis is that these storms are associated with appreciably higher rates of mentions focusing on the justices' ideology or some personal aspect—that is, the "cult of personality." Indeed, difference in means tests result in blindingly significant relationships for both Justice Blackmun ($|t| = 3.23$; $p < .001$) and Justice Stevens ($|t| = 3.39$; $p < .001$).[16] In a sense, then, it appears that the "cult of the robe" triggers references framing the "cult of personality." The two myths do not appear in isolation; more often than not, they appear together.

What effect this greater reference to the "cult of personality" has on the mass public's image of the justices—or, less directly, the Court—is an important analytical question. Given the timing of these media storms, this drumbeat of "cult of personality" mentions comes on the eve of the Court entering its summer recess. For the next three months, there will be only rare occasions where the media will have the opportunity to report on the Court performing its institutional and constitutional duties, and therefore rare occasions where reporting on the Court will be accompanied by references to its traditional symbols of institutional legitimacy. Instead, as we noted above, during the recess period, there is an even greater tendency to refer to the "cult of personality," at least when reporting on the individual justices, and it is reports on individual justices that likely are more common during this time period. Thus, for an extended amount of time, those paying attention to the Court will be exposed repeatedly to cues that do not necessarily contribute to the Court's institutional credibility. Instead, these cues put a human face (for good or ill) on the Court and its members. The frequency of these mentions, and the substantive nature of their content, are apt to arouse the interest of the reader, which in turn will contribute to the retention of this information (Graber 1984, 83, 87). Couple this with the tendency of individuals to drop information that is perceived as too remote and/or too complicated, and there is the beginning of a recipe for media storms on the justices to contribute to some decay in the Court's store of diffuse support.

At the same time, however, this decay, if it occurs, might not be uniform or substantial. First, most people probably do not pay enough attention to the media's reports on the Court or the justices to experience any real diminution in their deep and abiding levels of support for the Court, a support that is the product of socialization and therefore highly resistant to change. And second, as part of their diffuse support for the Court, individuals have an institutional schema about it comprising deeply embedded beliefs regarding the Court's proper behavior and the norms associated with it. This schema affects how information about the Court is processed. Cognitive balance theories suggest that "people avoid information that conflicts with knowledge, attitudes, and feelings that they already possess" (Graber 1984, 110). Given the generally deep levels of support the mass public has for the Court (Gibson and Caldeira 2009, 2011), it seems likely that people will generally avoid information that conflicts with this preexisting attitude.

Conclusion

From the preceding analysis and discussion, it seems clear that the press coverage of Justices Blackmun and Stevens (or at least that of the *New York Times*) provides a substantial amount of information about each individual justice across his career life cycle. Moreover, this coverage largely mirrors the broadcast coverage of Chief Justice Rehnquist (Diascro 2008). The information contained in this coverage, however, is left to the individual consumer of the news to acquire and process. And in that sense, the individual trying to deal with stories about the Court and its members in order to form opinions about the institution faces the same challenges as the issue voter—the information is "out there," but there is no guide to it and no guarantee that all the relevant information will be acquired or understood. In the end, then, we might ask: Substantively, what information does the *Times*'s coverage of Justices Blackmun and Stevens provide to the news consumer? The answer will vary across individuals, depending upon their attentiveness to the Court and its members.

100 The Personal Myth

TABLE 5.1 Three Types of Readers

Inattentive Reader	The inattentive reader does not subscribe to a national newspaper, perhaps not even to a state or local daily. He or she is unable to answer most general political knowledge questions correctly. He or she would not have an accurate sense of Blackmun's performance on the Bench, and to the degree this reader would be knowledgeable of Blackmun as a justice, it is because some aspects of Blackmun on the Court seeped into the broader social or cultural milieu (e.g., *Roe* and abortion).
Attentive Reader	The attentive reader subscribes to a national paper, and likely would know that the Senate has 100 members, and could identify the current chief justice, the vice president, and their own representative in the House. This reader would know the Supreme Court has nine justices, and in all likelihood he or she could identify several of them as well as several cases other than *Brown* and *Roe*. This reader's knowledge may not rise to that of instant or perfect recall, but when provided with prompts, he or she likely would answer correctly.
Very Attentive Reader	The very attentive reader reads the *New York Times* and quite possibly another paper on a daily basis. He or she listens to news radio and, these days, follows several news blogs. These readers know as much about the Court and the political system as does the attentive reader. In addition to historically salient cases, he or she could identify recent decisions that impacted current events. Given the name of a modern justice, this person could likely name the appointing president and hypothesize about the general ideology of each justice.

We approach this discussion in terms of three ideal types—the inattentive reader, the attentive reader, and the very attentive reader. The degree to which each ideal type understands each justice, given the media's coverage of him and the reader's likely awareness, defines each ideal type (see Table 5.1). We do not claim to have systematic data to analyze these ideal types and their information processing with respect to either justice. Instead, we use them as a device to explore and discuss the patterns of the *Times*'s coverage, as well as the overall substance of that coverage, that would be available to readers with different levels of interest and access to news sources.[17]

The Inattentive Reader

The inattentive reader would be characterized as unable to pass the typical battery of "U.S. Political Knowledge" questions. Accordingly, this reader is at a distinct disadvantage even if their news source is the "paper of record," the *New York*

Times.[18] With respect to the justices' tenures, our analysis shows that the *Times*'s coverage concentrates largely on retirement and resignation as the main event in each justice's career. (Of course, given the heated partisan politics surrounding Blackmun's nomination, substantial attention was given to it as well.) References to the individual justice apart from this major event are discrete and disjointed. Consequently, no casual reader will have a strong sense of Blackmun's or Stevens's performance on the Bench, his legal philosophy or ideological position, or even his voting record. To be sure, when mentioning individual justices, the business of the Court is emphasized. But even when reporting on opinion authorship or votes, there is rarely an effort to place these votes and opinions in a broader behavioral context.

For Blackmun, the inattentive reader likely will be aware of his ascension to the Bench, especially considering the context behind Blackmun's nomination. As discussed above, he was Nixon's third choice for the seat opened by Justice Fortas's resignation (a somewhat notable vacancy itself) after the debacles of the Carswell and Haynsworth nominations.[19] And this reader would likely have some basic knowledge of Blackmun's post-Court career (including his cameo role as Justice Story in the movie, *Amistad*), his retirement, and death. John Paul Stevens was perhaps the original "stealth" nominee, and it is unlikely an inattentive reader would have much familiarity with his confirmation.

Additionally, the inattentive reader may understand that Justice Blackmun had something to do with *Roe v. Wade*, given the media's consistent return to this topic as the issue began to dominate the legal political landscape—since 1980 abortion has figured prominently in nearly every major presidential election and nomination and confirmation battle for the Supreme Court, and increasingly in the lower federal courts. (John Paul Stevens was the last nominee to the Court *not* to be queried about the issue of abortion.) This bit of knowledge is assisted by the yearly protests on the anniversary of *Roe* outside the Supreme Court building that inevitably garner media attention and make reference to Blackmun. As was the case with their confirmations, Justice Stevens has no such "claim to fame" in terms of opinion authorship.

The Attentive Reader

Where we have established a baseline of knowledge accruing to the inattentive reader as if by osmosis, the attentive reader should be able to paint a more detailed picture of the justices and their work due to greater engagement with the news, although much information will be fleeting or incorrectly recalled. In other words, the attentive reader would be aware of this information around the time of coverage, but not retain the information throughout each justice's tenure or beyond. (Indeed, Graber notes that political information fades substantially without reinforcement, and even reinforcement provides only limited insulation (1984, 93).)

102 The Personal Myth

The attentive reader would be aware and have a greater grasp of all the information the inattentive reader possesses; in addition the attentive reader might recall some discrete pieces of personal information about the justices reported in the *Times*.

For example, the *Times* reported on the childhood friendship of Justice Blackmun and Chief Justice Burger, and this reader might recall the nickname given to them by the press—"The Minnesota Twins"—at least during Blackmun's confirmation and early years on the Bench. This reader might know that Justice Stevens was an adoptive parent, and that his son was arrested and charged with attempting to sell cocaine to an undercover agent.

With respect to decisions, the attentive reader would certainly know that Blackmun authored *Roe*, perhaps reading the long excerpts from Blackmun's opinion reprinted in the paper, and his subsequent defense of that decision in cases like *Akron, Webster v. Reproductive Services* (492 U.S. 490 [1989]), and *Planned Parenthood v. Casey* (505 U.S. 833 [1992]), all of which were discussed at some length beyond mere reporting of the individual decisions. This reader would also recognize that Justice Stevens was regularly a member of the shrinking pro-*Roe* majority in these decisions. The attentive reader would be aware of the justices' switch in position on the death penalty, and this same reader would have followed the coverage of the justices' advancing age. Finally, this reader would understand that each justice's tenure on the Court was lengthy and that they authored a great many opinions.

The Very Attentive Reader

The very attentive reader—the "wonk," the Court junkie, the trivia buff—would know even more details about the justices' lives and work, well beyond what the inattentive and attentive readers do. For example, the very attentive reader would be aware of various health issues confronting the justices as they aged. (Both justices were treated for prostate cancer: Blackmun in 1978 and 1988; Stevens in 1992.) This reader might be able to recall that Blackmun and Stevens, along with Justice Brennan, presided over a moot court at American University determining the true author of Shakespeare's plays. In the same "Briefing" the *Times* discusses "early handicapping" and notes that "Justice Blackmun is likely to be torn by the decision."[20] The *Times* later reported that the justices found for Shakespeare. The very attentive reader would probably know that Stevens was referred to as the "FedEx justice" early in his career because he would draft his opinions while at his home in Florida and then send them back and forth via Federal Express to his law clerks in Washington. (Eventually he became "the first telecommuting justice.")[21] Finally, this reader would have a sense of the justices' decisional behavior—the frequency of Stevens's dissents, concurrences, and special opinions; Blackmun's (and for that matter, Stevens's) migration from the conservative to the liberal end of the Court. This reader would also appreciate that upon Blackmun's resignation, Stevens assumed the mantle of the Court's chief liberal.

Regardless of a given reader's interest in the Court and/or access to information about it, the *Times* does not scrimp on reporting about the Court and its business, even when making references to individual justices. The *Times*'s reporting on Justices Blackmun and Stevens indicates that the business of the Court—with all the concomitant references to the legitimizing symbols associated with the "cult of the robe"—orients its coverage of these justices. This is not to say that the justices are presented solely as apolitical guardians of the Constitution and interpreters of that "sacred text." An appreciable proportion of mentions of the justices concern some aspect of what we identify as the "cult of personality," and these types of mentions are growing in frequency over time. Thus, as we found in the previous chapters, there seems to be a braiding of the two myths. How the public processes this dissonant information, of course, bears upon its image of the Court and in turn the Court's institutional legitimacy.

Notes

1 We used the following Boolean search phrases: (harry blackmun AND pub(new york times)) AND (justice OR judge) AND ftany(yes) AND NOT (Obituary OR Classified Ad OR Display Ad). (john paul stevens) AND pub(new york times)) AND (justice OR judge) AND ftany(yes) NOT (Obituary OR Classified Ad OR Display Ad).

2 Specifically, 15 mention codes were employed in the analysis. They are (1) vote with the majority, (2) vote with the minority, (3) majority opinion author, (4) dissenting opinion author, (5) concurring opinion author, (6) oral argument, (7) Court or institutional role, (8) personal, (9) ideology or legal philosophy, (10) abortion, (11) pre-Court career, (12) nomination / appointment / retirement, (13) non-merits decision, (14) didn't participate, and (15) other.

3 Our count of total *New York Times* articles is not a measure of *unique* articles on each justice. Since the tenures of Blackmun and Stevens overlapped for 20 terms, it is not unusual for an article to mention both justices.

4 "The Justice on His Colleagues," *New York Times*, February 20, 1983.

5 "Abortion Clinic on Special Alert," *New York Times*, January 17, 1985: A14.

6 Blackmun's family gave Greenhouse access to his papers six months prior to their public release. This early access resulted in her book, *Becoming Justice Blackmun*.

7 This relationship holds when second mentions are considered as well.

8 "On a Justice's Scale, Colleagues Are Sometimes Weighty," *New York Times*, July 24, 1988: B6.

9 Fred P. Graham, "Justices Narrow a Crime Decision by Warren Court," *New York Times*, February 24, 1971: 1.

10 The average age of the five justices in 1986 was 76.

11 Cynthia Gorny, "Justice Blackmun, Off the Record," *New York Times*, March 3, 1999: 15. This statement was not published until after the justice's death.

12 Specifically, the "work on the Court" categories are dissenting opinion author, majority opinion author, concurrence author, vote with the majority, dissent, cert./non-merits vote, institutional role of the Court, and didn't participate. The "non-work on the Court" categories are personal, ideology, abortion, nomination/appointment/retirement, pre-Court legal career, and other.

104 The Personal Myth

13 This nominal definition is a modification of Boydstun and her coauthors' definition of media storms: "an explosive increase in news coverage to a specific item . . . constituting a substantial share of the total news agenda during a certain time" (Boydstun, Hardy, and Walgrave 2012, 4–5). Coverage of any aspect of the Supreme Court is such a rare event we chose not to require our definition to include the component that the storm topic (here, an individual justice) constitutes "a substantial share of the total news agenda." A media storm is different from a news peg—to become a news peg, there is no required temporal longevity.

14 For Justice Blackmun, the full series mean is .209, and the rolling seven-day mean for a storm is 1.523. For Justice Stevens, the full series mean is .164; the rolling seven-day mean for a storm is 1.351.

15 Stories mentioning Blackmun or Stevens with respect to the Court's abortion decisions are the most frequent type of decision covered during the days identified as storms, but these stories account for only 6.8% of all the stories reporting the Court's outputs during the media storms, just a tick greater than stories reporting on free speech cases (6.3%).

16 These significantly higher rates of "cult of personality" mentions occur even when stories concerning the justices' appointment and retirement are excluded.

17 In Graber's seminal work on political information processing of the news, she relies on focus groups of 20 individuals that are composed of four types, arranged according to their interest in politics and access to the news (1984, see chapter 2).

18 We recognize that the inattentive reader is unlikely to subscribe to the *New York Times*; however, Diascro's work on Rehnquist and the broadcast media shows a similar pattern of information transmission (2008).

19 In fact, the *New York Times* reported on July 24, 1998, that Blackmun referred to himself as "old number three." This was a sobriquet he bestowed on Anthony Kennedy, Reagan's third nominee for Justice Powell's seat after Judge Bork was rejected and Judge Ginsburg withdrew. This was repeated in the *Times* in 2005. www.nytimes.com/2005/05/08/books/review/08KALMANL.html?pagewanted=all&_r=0 (last accessed June 20, 2013).

20 "Briefing," *New York Times*, September 19, 1987. Note this is one of the rare summer term stories. The case is revisited in the 2002 Term, after Blackmun's death, and the *Times* reminds us of his earlier participation in the original moot court (February 10, 2002).

21 Jeffrey Rosen, "The Dissenter Justice John Paul Stevens," *New York Times*, September 23, 2007: F50.

References

Althaus, Scott L., Jill A. Edy, and Patricia F. Phalen. 2001. "Using Substitutes for Full-Text News Stories in Content Analysis: Which Text Is Best?" *American Journal of Political Science* 45 (3):707–23.

Barnhart, Bill, and Gene Schlickman. 2010. *John Paul Stevens: An Independent Life*. DeKalb: Northern Illinois University Press.

Blasi, Victor, ed. 1983. *The Burger Court and the Counter-Revolution that Wasn't*. New Haven, CT: Yale University Press.

Boydstun, Amber, Anne Hardy, and Stefaan Walgrave. 2012. "Two Faces of Media Attention: Media Stroms vs. General Coverage." In *Media, Movements, and Politics*. Antwerp, Belgium: Universiteit Antwerpen.

Davis, Richard. 2011. *Justices and Journalists: The U.S. Supreme Court and the Media*. New York: Cambridge University Press.

Diascro, Jennifer Segal. 2008. "The Legacy of Chief Justice Rehnquist: A View from the Small Screen." *Judicature* 92:106–17.

Gibson, James L., and Gregory A. Caldeira. 2009. *Citizens, Courts, and Confirmations: Positivity Theory and the Judgments of the American People*. Princeton, NJ: Princeton University Press.

———. 2011. "Has Legal Realism Damaged the Legitimacy of the U.S. Supreme Court?" *Law and Society Review* 45 (1):195–219.

Graber, Doris A. 1984. *Processing the News: How People Tame the Information Tide*. New York: Longman.

Slotnick, Elliot E., and Jennifer A. Segal. 1998. *Television News and the Supreme Court: All the News That's Fit to Print*. New York: Cambridge University Press.

Solberg, Rorie L., and Eric N. Waltenburg. 2014. "Constructing Harry Blackmun." In *Covering the United States Supreme Court in the Digital Age*, pp. 109–125. ed. R. Davis. New York: Oxford University Press.

Spill, Rorie L., and Zoe M. Oxley. 2003. "Philosopher Kings or Political Actors: How the Media Portray the Supreme Court." *Judicature* 87 (1):23–29.

6

CONCLUSION: PROCESSING THE MYTHS OF THE COURT

The basic question motivating the research presented in this book is how does the modern, mainstream media portray the U.S. Supreme Court? It is our contention that the media—through its selection of what to cover about the Court and what to emphasize in that coverage—has ushered in an image of the Court as a more political and polarized institution, an institution affected by the personalities on the Bench and their individual policy preferences. And this has implications. Accordingly, the media's focus on certain events intrinsic to the Court (nominations and confirmations), certain types of decisions rendered by the Court (civil liberties and rights), as well as the media's determination of which moments in the career life cycles of the justices (retirements) and which attributes about them are especially newsworthy yields an inaccurate (at best) or even warped perception of the Court and its business. This perception in turn might bear upon the public's attitude toward the Court.[1]

In chapter 1 we reviewed the elements of the traditional legal myth of the Court and discussed how this myth contributes to the Court's deep reservoir of institutional credibility with the mass public. Political myths, in general, are important; they encourage confidence in and fealty to the political system, its institutions, and its outputs. And perhaps no institution is better served by, or more dependent upon, its myth than is the U.S. Supreme Court. Lacking the power to compel, it can only persuade, and the broad-based belief among the public that the Court is apolitical and that the justices "suspend . . . [their] biases, values, attachments, and preferences in the pursuit of objective legal decisions" (Scheb and Lyons 2000) adds mightily to the Court's persuasive capacity. Indeed, as Gibson and Caldeira note, it is when the Court ceases to be perceived as a "uniquely nonpolitical political institution" that its institutional support is imperiled (2011, 200).

We then turned our attention to the collection of norms that traditionally have encouraged the press to enshrine the legal myth in its coverage of the Court. And finally we discussed the modern journalistic norms of personalization, drama, and novelty (Boykoff and Boykoff 2007, 1192) as well as a variety of developments—the Court's involvement in some of the most socially and politically divisive issues of the times, the increasing presence and activity of organized interests, the change in the nomination and confirmation process, and even the greater willingness of some justices to "go public"—that have helped to usher in a new myth, one emphasizing politics and personalities.

In chapter 2 we began our systematic analysis. Here, we showed the media's coverage of the four most recent confirmation hearings was skewed. Where the Senate confirmation hearings saw the Senate inquisitors and nominees largely adhering to questions and responses emphasizing the "cult of the robe" and federal power, the media chose to emphasize the "cult of personality" and to employ quotations from the senators to characterize the politics and machinations of the confirmation process. The press also chose to replace the senators' emphasis on the issue of federal power with the more controversial (and presumably interesting) social issues of discrimination and abortion. As a result, the consumer of the media's reports on the confirmation hearings would be fairly well informed about any compelling personal histories of the nominee (thereby contributing to the attention paid to personality), but also left with the impression that most of the genuinely consequential business before the Court concerns the issues of discrimination and privacy, especially as it relates to abortion. More importantly, in the justices' introduction to the mass public through the media's coverage of their confirmation hearings, the "cult of personality" is clearly present.

The media's concentration on certain types of cases in its confirmation coverage is repeated in its coverage of the Court's decisions. In chapter 3 we found that the media appreciably overreport decisions concerning civil rights and liberties issues, thereby leaving the impression that the Court's agenda largely is composed of this broad issue domain. As a result, the news consumer will be left with the sense that the Court is involved with and speaks to only a very small subset of the political questions and controversies confronting the nation. Furthermore, we found that not only does the media overreport decisions dealing with civil rights and liberties, it does so by concentrating on particular cases in that issue domain. Importantly, we showed that as the number of stories associated with a given decision increased, there was also a significant increase in the average number of sentences per story mentioning the decision's political justification and/or its political implications. As a result, the media's tendency to concentrate on certain decisions in the civil rights and liberties issue domain makes it much more likely for the reader or viewer to come into contact with the "cult of personality."

In chapter 4 we continued to explore the media's tendency to focus its coverage of the Court's outputs on both certain issue domains and unique cases within

108 Processing the Myths of the Court

those issue domains. Here, we take up the media's reporting of salient "landmark" cases. First, we find that the media does a good job of identifying landmark cases for coverage. Overall, every landmark decision has at least one story devoted to it among our four media outlets, and many of the decisions (52%) have enough stories to achieve "news peg" status. Even among this subset of uniformly high-consequence decisions, however, the media is prone to emphasize certain issue domains—namely, the First Amendment, civil rights, and privacy. It also bears noting that given the high incidence of stories on the landmark cases being written by staff reporters, consumers of the news are more likely to be exposed to the "cult of personality" in the coverage of these decisions.

In chapter 5 we shifted our attention from the media's coverage of the Court's decisions to its coverage of the individual justice. Specifically, we explored the incidence and nature of *New York Times* mentions of Justices Harry Blackmun and John Paul Stevens. We found that the bulk of the first mentions of the justices in the *Times* concerned their behavior with respect to Court decisions (i.e., their authorship of opinions or their votes), but that those stories that provided more news about the justices (i.e., stories with second and third mentions) contained appreciable references to the justices' ideological or legal positions as well as personal information on them. We also found that these references to the "cult of personality" increase significantly in the stories reporting on the crush of decisions handed down as the Court's term comes to an end. This indicates that references associated with the "cult of personality" oftentimes occur simultaneously with references that invoke the traditional legal myth associated with the Court.

Happily, nowhere did we find the legal myth, the "cult of the robe," with its associated legitimizing symbolism, excised from the modern media's coverage of the Court. What we did find was a tendency for the "cult of the robe" to share column inches and broadcast airtime with the "cult of personality." (We also presented some evidence suggesting that this tendency is increasing over time.) In short, the mass public, as consumers of the news, is being provided with dissonant images of the Court. And this prompts the questions: How does the individual consumer of the news process this discordant information? Which myth is more likely to resonate? And might this make any difference to the institutional support for the Court among the mass public? The answers to these questions are beyond our data, but we can offer some informed speculation.

In her seminal study on how the public processes the news, Graber found that people are more apt to attend to and recall news stories about which they derive some personal pleasure. Most common to these stories is information concerning "human interest elements . . . and [information] relevant to personal life-style" (1984, 86). The individual news consumer is appreciably less likely to process stories for information pertaining to broader society or governmental affairs. As Graber puts it, the "Societal significance of the story was . . . a comparatively minor attraction" (1984, 86). This suggests that when it comes to coverage of the Court, the typical consumer of the news will be more likely to process stories containing elements of the "cult of personality," and information comprising that portrayal of the Court and its members will have greater significance to the individual. After all, the "cult of personality" emphasizes human-interest features, the personal lifestyles of the justices, and the ideological divide on the bench.

Furthermore, this attention to the personal may be even more acute when processing news about the Court as opposed to political news generally. Graber found that while individuals actively select certain types of information, they also purposefully exclude other types of information from their consideration. Specifically, individuals are apt to reject information that is especially remote or complicated (1984, 89–90), and remote and complicated information is part and parcel of many stories reporting on the Court and its outputs. The Court itself is an insular and mysterious institution, refusing to provide simple and direct explanations for its decisions. The disputes before it often involve litigants with whom the individual has little or nothing in common (e.g., huge multinational corporations, states). And the reasoning for the Court's decisions (its policy pronouncements) rests upon sophisticated legal conclusions that may be decipherable only to highly trained legal professionals. Consequently, when confronted with the dissonant information on the Court that we have found to be contained in more and more stories, it seems likely that the individual will process and retain the information consistent with the "cult of personality," while choosing to exclude the more remote and complicated information associated with the "cult of the robe." And as a result, aspects of the "cult of personality" will compose a greater share of the attribute agenda of the Court (on "attribute agendas," see McCombs 2005, 160–61).

Might this make any difference to the Court as an institution? As an institution and in the short run, the answer is probably no. Institutionally, the Court enjoys a deep reservoir of diffuse support among the mass public, although there is notable variation among members of the public (see Caldeira and Gibson 1992; Clawson and Waltenburg 2009; Gibson and Caldeira 1993). This type of support is the product of political socialization, and therefore is not given to abrupt and seismic changes (Easton 1965; on the stability of the Court's diffuse support, see Clawson and Waltenburg 2009; Gibson et al. 2003). To the extent media portrayals can affect such deeply rooted and enduring attitudes, those portrayals must be sustained "over relatively long periods of time" (Bartels 1993, 275). In other words, the new myth may begin to erode the Court's institutional credibility among individuals, but the time horizon is quite distant before this erosion would become consequential. Even more on point, it is not clear that the media's increasing focus on the effect of the justices' ideological proclivities on their decisions is *necessarily* damaging the Court's image in the eyes of the public. Gibson and Caldeira (2011) have presented empirical evidence showing that the public's awareness that ideology and partisan preferences affect the justices' decisional behavior does not erode

110 Processing the Myths of the Court

the Court's institutional credibility. They suggest that this is a consequence of the perception that the justices exercise these "political" forces in a principled manner, and that the presence of the "cult of the robe," with its legitimizing symbols of objectivity and fairness, *alongside* the "cult of personality" helps to maintain the perception that the justices are engaging in principled decision making.

In the long run, however, the increasingly frequent presence of the "cult of personality" in the media's reporting on the Court might begin to have a deleterious effect on its institutional credibility and its ability to persuade in at least three ways. First, elements of the "cult of personality" may be composing a larger share of the public's "attribute agenda" with respect to the Court. In our data, it appears with greater regularity in media stories on the Court over time. Thus, politics and personalities, preferences and ideologies are what the consumers of the news are apt to *think about* the Court more and more. As we have pointed out, the Court gets into trouble when it loses its unique status as a "nonpolitical political institution" (Gibson and Caldeira 2011, 200). To be sure, simply reporting that ideologies and preferences affect the justices' decisions does not damn the Court in the eyes of the public (Gibson and Caldeira 2011). But should those reports occur without the inoculating effects of the legal myth, either because the stories do not contain references to the "cult of the robe" or those references are not processed and recalled, the Court's institutional credibility will erode. Indeed, Clawson and Waltenburg (2009) have shown that exposure to the minority press's coverage of the Supreme Court—with its emphasis on the political implications for minority populations of the Court's decisions and its relatively infrequent references to the legal myth surrounding the Court—is negatively related to diffuse support (for similar findings, see also Christenson and Glick 2014; Johnston and Bartels 2010; Nie and Waltenburg 2014).

Second and relatedly, the media's growing emphasis on the "cult of personality" in its reporting on the Court may effectively "crowd out" references to many of the symbols of judicial legitimacy that are part and parcel of traditional coverage—the use of the title "justice," the unique dress (robes), the temple-like Supreme Court building. Recent work by Gibson, Lodge, and Woodson (2012) has shown that the presence of these symbols has something of a priming effect, bringing to mind the legitimacy and credibility of the Court itself. As a result, when stories on a Court decision include the symbols of legitimacy, there is a greater likelihood the individual will perceive an action of the Court as legitimate, even if the individual does not agree with it (see also Gibson and Nelson 2014).

Finally, generational replacement may result in cohorts less deeply committed to the Court than their elders. The dynamic might work something like this. Where earlier generations experienced a relatively steady drumbeat of reinforcing messages concerning the Court's unique nature, individuals coming to political maturity now are not as likely to be treated consistently to reports that the Court is different. Consequently, these generations do not see their running tally of support for the Court bolstered through the media. Inevitably, the Court will disappoint, and as debits are made, the reservoir of support for the Court is neither as rapidly nor as fully replenished.

One final point deserves some mention. Namely, it is not simply *what* is reported about the justices' actions but *how* those actions are reported that matters. That politics, preferences, and ideologies affect the justices' decisions does not undermine the Court's diffuse support *so long as those decisions are perceived as principled*. However, if those decisional forces were consistently framed in a way that suggests the justices behave strategically, the Court's institutional credibility would likely be undercut. Indeed, Hibbing and Theiss-Morse suggest an explanation for the Court's relatively high levels of institutional support among the public is that the Court's decisional processes—any give-and-take among the justices, any bargaining or deal-cutting—is not reported (1995, 58; see also Ramirez 2008). Certainly, in the short run, it seems likely that public support for a given decision where strategic considerations were reported would be affected (see, for example, Clawson and Waltenburg 2002 on the effects of media framing on public support for a Court decision). To the extent, then, that the politics involved in the justices' decisional behavior are covered, or that the recipe for judicial sausage is reported (to borrow and adapt a legislative metaphor), the institutional credibility of the Court may suffer. That recipe, however, remains a tightly guarded secret, one the justices are unlikely to share.

In the first decades of the twenty-first century, the justices continue to focus public and press attention on their opinions while maintaining tight control over information concerning their decisional processes. In no small part this has been due to the belief that concealing the process contributes to the institution's public esteem (Davis 2011, 194–95). Yet, the justices have also become more willing to engage the press and are more likely to present themselves to the public. Davis (2011) points out that they do so for a variety of reasons—to defend the institution, to shape the debate concerning public policy, and to affect public opinion about themselves and their colleagues. In the process, however, they may be sowing the seeds for the demise of the Court's position in the public eye. As we have shown, the modern, mainstream press has begun to concentrate on the politics of the Court and the personalities of the justices. In other words, the media is covering the Court and the justices more like it covers the other institutions of government. And as Davis notes, "If the frame for press coverage of the justices is similar to that of other government figures, the result may be lower public regard for the Court as a legitimate arbiter. The result could be harmful to the Court" (2011, 194).

Note

1 Indeed in Solberg's *Judicial Process and Politics* course (Winter 2014), the students took exception to Baum's characterization of the rate of unanimous decisions—". . . only

a minority of decisions are unanimous—42 percent in the 2009–2010 term" (Baum 2013, 12). They commented on why he would use the word "only." Their perception based upon coverage of the Court was that it was rarely unified and deeply divided. Solberg was deeply gratified to have her students unwittingly support the premise of this work, and upon being informed of the perception of Solberg's class, so too was Waltenburg.

References

Bartels, Larry M. 1993. "Messages Received: The Political Impact of Media Exposure." *American Political Science Review* 87 (2):267–85.

Baum, Lawrence. 2013. *American Courts: Process and Policy.* 7th ed. Boston: Wadsworth, Cengage Learning.

Boykoff, Maxwell T., and Jules M. Boykoff. 2007. "Climate Change and Journalistic Norms: A Case-Study of U.S. Mass-Media Coverage." *Geoforum* 38 (6):1190–204.

Caldeira, Gregory A., and James L. Gibson. 1992. "The Etiology of Public Support for the Supreme Court." *American Journal of Political Science* 36:635–64.

Christenson, Dino P., and David M. Glick. 2014. "Roberts' Health Care Decision Disrobed: The Microfoundations of the Court's Legitimacy." Working paper, Boston University.

Clawson, Rosalee A., and Eric N. Waltenburg. 2002. "Support for a Supreme Court Affirmative Action Decision: A Story in Black and White." *American Politics Research* 31:251–79.

———. 2009. *Legacy and Legitimacy: Black Americans and the Supreme Court.* Philadelphia: Temple University Press.

Davis, Richard. 2011. *Justices and Journalists: The U.S. Supreme Court and the Media.* New York: Cambridge University Press.

Easton, David. 1965. *A Systems Analysis of Political Life.* New York: Wiley.

Gibson, James L., and Gregory A. Caldeira. 1993. "Blacks and the U.S. Supreme Court: Models of Diffuse Support." *Journal of Politics* 54:1120–45.

———. 2011. "Has Legal Realism Damaged the Legitimacy of the U.S. Supreme Court?" *Law and Society Review* 45 (1):195–219.

Gibson, James L., Gregory A. Caldeira, and Lester Kenyatta Spence. 2003. "The Supreme Court and the U.S. Presidential Election of 2000: Wounds, Self-Inflicted or Otherwise?" *British Journal of Political Science* 33:535–56.

Gibson, James L., Milton Lodge, and Benjamin Woodson. 2012. "The Symbols of Legitimacy: Thinking, Fast and Slow, About the U.S. Supreme Court." Paper presented at the annual meeting of the *American Political Science Association.* New Orleans.

Gibson, James L., and Michael J. Nelson. 2014. "Change in Institutional Support for the U.S. Supreme Court: Is the Court's Legitimacy Imperiled by the Decisions It Makes?" Working paper, Washington University in St. Louis.

Graber, Doris A. 1984. *Processing the News: How People Tame the Information Tide.* New York: Longman.

Hibbing, John R., and Elizabeth Theiss-Morse. 1995. *Congress as Public Enemy: Public Attitudes Toward American Political Institutions.* New York: Cambridge University Press.

Johnston, Christopher D., and Brandon L. Bartels. 2010. "Sensationalism and Sobriety: Differential Media Exposure and Attitudes Toward American Courts." *Public Opinion Quarterly* 74 (2):260–86.

McCombs, Maxwell. 2005. "The Agenda-Setting Function of the Press." In *The Press*, pp. 156–168. ed. G. Overholser and K. H. Jamieson. New York: Oxford University Press.

Nie, Mintao, and Eric N. Waltenburg. 2014. "Media Impact on Diffuse Support for the Supreme Court: The Black Media." Paper presented at the annual meeting of the *Midwest Political Science Association*. Chicago.

Ramirez, Mark D. 2008. "Procedural Perceptions and Support for the U.S. Supreme Court." *Political Psychology* 29 (5):675–98.

Scheb, John M., and William Lyons. 2000. "The Myth of Legality and Public Evaluation of the Supreme Court." *Social Science Quarterly* 81 (4):928–40.

INDEX

ABC television news 16, 54n4
abortion 4, 8, 33, 49, 86, 87, 89, 97, 101,
    104n14, 107; Blackmun and mentions
    of 94–5; landmark decision(s) and 68,
    70, 73, 80; substantive issue category 17,
    21, 23, 28, 30–2, 103n2, 103n12; *see also*
    privacy
Advertiser 16, 18, 34n7; *see also* nomination
    and confirmation process
Advocate 16, 18, 20, 34n7; *see also*
    nomination and confirmation process
affirmative action 66–8, 74, 80, 82; *see also*
    discrimination
Agostini v. Felton 76–7
Alito, Samuel 5, 8, 16–20, 22–3, 30, 32,
    34n5, 34n11, 34n15, 50, 55n9
Amistad 101
Arizona v. Roberson 75
*Astroline Communications Co. v. Schurberg
    Broadcasting of Hartford, Inc.* 74
attentive reader 100–2; *see also* inattentive
    reader; very attentive reader
attribute agenda 109–10

Batson v. Kentucky 67–8
Biden, Joseph (Joe) 23, 26
Bipartisan Campaign Reform Act 82
Blackmun, Harry 4, 9, 68, 70; *New York
    Times* mentions of 85–90, 92–3, 95–9,
    101–3, 103n3, 103n6, 104n14, 104n15,
    104n19, 104n20, 108

*Board of Education of the Westside Community
    Schools (District 66) v. Mergens* 72
Bork, Robert 13–14, 26, 33n3, 104n19
*Bowen, Secretary of Health and Human
    Services v. American Hospital Ass'n, et al.*
    69–70
Bowsher v. Synar 68
Brandeis, Louis 33n3, 68
Brennan, William 67, 73–4, 102
Brown v. Board of Education 65, 81, 89
Buckley v. Valeo 48, 64
Burger, Warren 54n3, 65, 69–70, 95, 102
Bush, George H. W. 14
Bush, George W. 3, 15, 16, 81
*Butler v. Kenneth D. McKellar,
    Warden et al.* 75

*Cable Television Consumer Protection and
    Competition Act* 77
California v. Usery 50
Carelli, Richard 5; *see also* Court reporters
*Carla A. Hills, Secretary of Housing and
    Urban Development v. Gautreaux* 49, 66
Carswell, G. Harrold 94, 101
CBS Evening News 16, 38, 41, 47–8, 51–3,
    54n4, 66, 70, 79–80
*Citizens United v. Federal Election
    Commission* 5, 50, 82
*City of Akron v. Akron Center for
    Reproductive Health* 94–5
City of Boerne v. Flores 76–7, 79

116 Index

City of Renton v. Playtime Theatres 69–70
civil rights 19, 39, 46–7, 64–70, 75–6,
79–80, 107–8
Civil Rights Act 68, 80
Clean Air Act 49, 81
Clinton, William (Bill) 14, 30, 78, 84n7
Clinton v. Jones 49, 78–9
Code of Conduct for Supreme Court Law
Clerks 12
Concerned Alumni of Princeton (CAP) 17
confirmation *see* nomination and
confirmation process
*Congressional Quarterly Guide to the
Supreme Court* 58, 66; *see also* landmark
decision(s)
Cornyn, John 26
Court reporters 3, 33, 52, 55n12, 58, 64; *see
also* staff reporters; wire service reporters
*CQ Guide see Congressional Quarterly Guide
to the Supreme Court*
criminal procedure 39, 46, 63–7, 69–70,
72, 74–6, 79, 83
*Cruzan v. Director, Missouri Department of
Health* 73–4
cult of personality: defined 4; effect on
Court's legitimacy 110–13; forces
contributing to rise of 5–6, 107;
increasing tendency toward 51–2, 93;
journalistic norms and practices and
4–5, 107; landmark decision(s) and 50,
57, 64, 71, 83, 84, 108; media storms and
98–9, 104n16, 108; news processing
and 109; nominations and confirmations
and 13, 21, 23–4, 27–30, 32, 33, 107; *see
also* new myth; political myth
cult of the robe 46, 51, 54, 85; continued
presence of 92, 98, 103, 108; defined
1–2, 106; effect on Court's legitimacy
2, 110; forces contributing to 2–4; news
processing and 109; nominations and
confirmations and 13, 17, 20–1, 23–4,
27–9, 32, 107; *see also* legal myth; myth
of legality

Davis, Richard 3, 5–6, 12–13, 33n1, 33n3,
52–3, 87, 89, 93, 111
death penalty 63–4, 67, 102
Denniston, Lyle 40, 55n12, 82; *see also*
Court reporters
diffuse support 99, 109–11; *see also*
institutional credibility; institutional
support; legitimacy

discrimination 17, 21, 30–1, 33, 34n13,
49, 66–8, 76, 80, 107; *see also* affirmative
action
doctor-assisted suicide 97; *see also*
euthanasia; physician-assisted suicide;
right to die
due process 39, 46, 64, 67, 75, 77, 83
Due Process Clause 77–8, 82

economic activity 39, 74, 76, 78, 82–3
Eighth Amendment 63–4, 79
*Employment Division, Department of Human
Resources of Oregon v. Smith* 72
Environmental Protection Agency (EPA)
21, 49, 81–2
Equal Access Act 72
Equal Protection Clause 67, 77; *see also*
Free Exercise Clause; free exercise of
religion
Establishment Clause 72, 75, 77
euthanasia 77–8; *see also* doctor-assisted
suicide; physician-assisted suicide; right
to die
Evaluator 16, 18, 20, 23, 34n7; *see
also* nomination and confirmation
process
exclusionary rule 65–6

FEC v. Wisconsin Right to Life 81–2
federalism 50, 76, 78
Federalists 14
federal power 17, 21, 23, 27–8, 30–1, 79,
107
Feingold, Russell (Russ) 26, 34n15
Feinstein, Dianne 26, 28
Fifth Amendment 75
First Amendment 39, 46–7, 50, 64–5,
69–77, 79, 81–3, 108
Flag Desecration Law 71
Flag Protection Act 49, 71–2
Ford, Gerald 94
Ford v. Wainwright 67
Fortas, Abe 14, 101
Fourth Amendment 65, 74–5
Free Exercise Clause 75; *see also*
Establishment Clause; free exercise of
religion
free exercise of religion 71–2, 77; *see also*
Establishment Clause; Free Exercise
Clause
French v. Rutan 73
Furman v. Georgia 64

Ginsburg, Ruth Bader 3, 34n5, 78
Gonzales v. Carhart 49, 80, 82
Graber, Doris 52, 101, 104n17, 108–9; *see also* news processing
Graham, Fred 92; *see also* Court reporters
Graham, Lindsey 26–7, 29, 34n15
Gramm-Rudman-Hollings Deficit Control Act 68
Greenhouse, Linda 53, 79, 87, 89, 103n6; *see also* Court reporters
Gregg v. Georgia 48, 64–5
Griswold v. Connecticut 68
Grutter v. Bolinger 80–1

Hatch, Orrin 3, 19, 30, 34n11
Haynsworth, Clement 94, 101
Hodgson v. Minnesota 73
Hughes, Charles Evans 2
Hurricane Katrina 17

ideology 14, 51–2, 90, 92, 98, 103n2, 103n12, 109; *see also* cult of personality
inattentive reader 100–2, 104n18; *see also* attentive reader; very attentive reader
institutional credibility 9, 99, 106, 109–11; *see also* diffuse support; institutional support; legitimacy
institutional support 54, 106, 108, 111; *see also* diffuse support; institutional credibility; legitimacy
interest groups 13, 15, 33n3, 81, 107; *see also* nomination and confirmation process; organized interests
Internal Revenue Service (IRS) 66

Jeffersonian-Republicans 14
Jimmy Swaggart Ministries v. Board of Equalization of California 75
Johnson, Andrew 14
Johnson, Lyndon 14
journalistic norms 4, 64, 107
judicial philosophy 13, 15, 17, 20, 23, 27, 29–30, 33; *see also* cult of the robe; legal myth; myth of legality
Judiciary Act of 1801 14
Judiciary Committee 8, 15–18, 22–3, 25–6; *see also* nominations and confirmations
Jurek v. Texas 64

Kagan, Elena 3, 8, 16–17, 19–20, 22–3, 29–31, 34n5
Kennedy, Anthony 71, 77, 80, 104n19
Kennedy, Edward (Ted) 18, 23, 26
Kyl, Jon 26

landmark case(s) *see* landmark decision(s)
landmark decision(s) 8, 57–8, 63–72, 74, 76, 78–80, 82–3, 83n2, 83n3, 108
Lawrence v. Texas 68
Leahy, Patrick 21–2, 26, 34n15
Ledbetter, Lily 80
Ledbetter v. Goodyear Tire & Rubber Co. 80
Leegin Creative Leather Products v. PSKS 82
legal myth 2–3, 6–7, 13, 54, 106–8, 110; *see also* cult of the robe; myth of legality
legitimacy 2, 4, 7, 83, 98, 103, 109–11; *see also* diffuse support; institutional credibility; institutional support
Lily Ledbetter Fair Pay Act 80
Local 28 of the Sheet Metal Workers International Ass'n v. EEOC 67
Local 93 of the International Ass'n of Firefighters v. City of Cleveland 67
Lockhart v. McCree 67
Los Angeles Times 38, 41, 47–50, 52, 54n6, 58, 66, 69–70, 74–5, 79, 82

Massachusetts v. Environmental Protection Agency 49, 81–2
media storm 97–9, 104n13, 104n15
Metro Broadcasting Inc. v. FCC 74
Michelin Tire Corp. v. Wages 49
Michigan Department of State Police v. Sitz 74
Midnight Appointments 14
Minnesota Twins 102; *see also* Harry Blackmun; Warren Burger
Minnesota v. Hodgson 73
Miranda protections 92
Missouri v. Jenkins 75–6
Morris, Gouvernur 14
Morse v. Frederick 81
Murphy, Frank 3
myth of legality 1–3, 12; *see also* cult of the robe; legal myth

National League of Cities v. Usery 49–50, 65
NBC television news 16, 29, 35n21, 54n4, 93
Nebraska Press Ass'n v. Stuart 65, 69

118 Index

new myth 4, 8–9, 13, 107, 109; *see also* cult of personality; political myth
news peg 4, 48–50, 57–8, 65–70, 74, 76, 79, 82–3, 83n1, 104n13, 108
news processing 104n17, 108–9; *see also* Doris Graber
New York Times 16, 38, 41, 47–9, 52, 57–8, 66, 70, 74–5, 79–80, 82, 85–8, 89, 93, 95, 97, 99, 108
Nixon, Richard 14, 92, 94, 101
nomination *see* nomination and confirmation process
nomination and confirmation process 3–4, 6, 8, 13, 14–15, 18, 22, 26, 33n2, 33n3, 34n8, 85–6, 92, 94, 97, 101, 106–7; *see also* cult of personality; cult of the robe

Obama, Barack 3, 5, 16, 20, 26, 34n9, 50, 55n9, 80
Obamacare *see Patient Protection and Affordable Care Act*
O'Connor, Sandra Day 33n2, 73, 77, 94
Ohio v. Akron Center for Reproductive Health 74
Olmstead v. United States 68
O'Neill v. Synar 68
organized interests 5–6, 107; *see also* interest groups; nomination and confirmation process
Osborne v. Ohio 75

Parents Involved in Community Schools v. Seattle School District No. 1 80, 82
Partial Birth Abortion Act 80
partisan 16, 18–20, 34n6; *see also* nomination and confirmation process
partisanship 14–15, 19, 24, 38; *see also* cult of personality
Pasadena v. Spangler 65
Patient Protection and Affordable Care Act 4
Phillip Morris USA v. Williams 82
physician-assisted suicide 49, 77–8, *see also* doctor-assisted suicide; euthanasia; right to die
Planned Parenthood v. Casey 95, 105
political implications 50, 53, 69, 85, 107, 110; *see also* cult of personality; new myth; political justifications
political justifications 50–2, 107; *see also* cult of personality; new myth; political implications
political myth 2, 106; *see also* cult of personality; new myth

Powell, Lewis 70, 104n19
Press Characterization of the Hearing 17, 28
Press-Enterprise Co. v. Superior Court of California 69–70
Printz v. United States 78–9, 83n3
privacy 4–5, 8, 18, 46–7, 50, 64, 66, 68, 70, 73, 75–80, 83n3, 107–8; *see also* abortion
procedure 17, 21–3
Proffit v. Florida 64
Proquest Historical Newspapers archive 86

qualifications 13–15, 17, 21–3, 28, 33; *see also* nomination and confirmation process

Radical Republicans 14
rational basis test 78
Reagan, Ronald 14–16, 26, 35n22, 69, 94, 104n19
Reconstruction 14
Rehabilitation Act 69
Rehnquist, William 3, 14, 16–17, 22, 34n5, 54n3, 65, 70, 76, 99, 104n18
Rehnquist Court 30, 50, 76, 78
Religious Freedom and Restoration Act 77
Reno v. ACLU 76
Richardson & Walker v. McKnight 79
right to die 73, 78; *see also* doctor-assisted suicide; euthanasia; physician-assisted suicide
Roberts, John 3–4, 8, 15–23, 30–2, 34n5, 34n14, 34n15, 53, 54n3, 80–1
Roberts, Owen 2
Roberts Court 30
Roberts v. Louisiana 65
Roe v. Wade 4, 8, 68, 73, 87, 89, 94–6, 101–2; *see also* abortion; Harry Blackmun; privacy
Rutan v. Republican Party of Illinois 73

Savage, David 58; *see also Congressional Quarterly Guide to the Supreme Court*; Court reporters
Scalia, Antonin 15
Schumer, Charles (Chuck) 26, 34n14, 34n18
search and seizure 74
Search and Seizure Clause 75
Senate hearings 4, 8, 13, 14–33, 33n2, 34n7, 34n10, 34n11, 34n12, 107; *see also* individual justices; nomination and confirmation process

Index **119**

Senate v. Synar 68
Sessions, Jefferson (Jeff) 23
Shakespeare, William 102
Sherman Antitrust Act 82
Sixth Amendment 67
Smith v. Goguen 72
Sotomayor, Sonia 8, 16–17, 19–20, 22–3, 26, 28–9, 31–2, 34n5
Southern strategy 14
Spaeth, Harold 63; *see also Supreme Court Database*
Spallone v. United States 75–6
Specter, Arlen 18
Spence v. Washington 72
staff reporters 52–3, 58, 64, 70, 79, 108; *see also* Court reporters; wire service reporters
Stanley v. Georgia 75
Stenberg v. Carhart 80
Stevens, John Paul 5, 9, 70, 81; *New York Times* mentions of 85–7, 89–91, 93–9, 101–3, 103n3, 104n14, 104n15, 108
Stone v. Powell 65
Story, Joseph 101
Street v. New York 72
strict scrutiny doctrine 72, 77
Supreme Court docket 38–50, 57, 68, 76, 80, 82
Supreme Court Database 39, 46, 71
symbols of legitimacy 98, 103, 110; *see also* cult of the robe; diffuse support; institutional credibility; institutional support; legal myth; legitimacy; myth of legality

Takings Clause 83
Taylor, Stuart 88; *see also* Court reporters

Texas v. Johnson 71–2
Thomas, Clarence 14, 34n5
Thompson, James 73
Thornburgh v. American College of Obstetricians and Gynecologists 68, 73, 95
Tinker v. Des Moines 81
Turner Broadcasting System v. FCC 76–7

United States v. Eichman 49, 71, 74, 78
United States v. Janis 66
United States v. O'Hagan 78
United States v. Verdugo-Urquidez 75
USA Today 16
U.S. Supreme Court Database see Supreme Court Database
U.S. v. Butler 3

Vacco v. Quill 78–9
Vasquez v. Hillery 67–8
very attentive reader 102; *see also* attentive reader; inattentive reader
Voting Rights Act 77

war on terror 30
Washington Post 16, 26, 29, 38, 41, 47–9, 52, 54n6, 66, 70, 74–5, 79, 82
Washington v. Glucksberg 49, 78–9
Webster v. Reproductive Services 102
White, Byron R. 5, 68
wire service reporters 52, 64, 89; *see also* Court reporters; staff reporters
wise Latina 17, 20, 23
Wolff v. Rice 65
Woodson v. North Carolina 64–5
Wyatt v. Cole 79
Wygant v. Jackson Board of Education 67–8